With a full heart and deepest thanks to

MAHARISHI MAHESH YOGI

Acknowledgments

___

I want to express my deepest thanks to several people:

To my wife, Rita, and my children, Gautama and Mallika, for their faith, tolerance, and love.

To my editor, Ruth Hapgood, for her good humor, patience, and much-valued advice.

To Muriel Nellis and Carla Linton, who performed many expert, kind services at every stage.

To Huntley Dent, whose deep friendship and extraordinary literary skills continue to guide my every effort.

Contents

—

Dark Night in New Jersey

"DOCTOR, we need you on Surgical Four," a nurse's voice said over the phone. "We've had an expiration."

"A what?" I asked.

"An expiration," she carefully repeated, "on Surgical Four. We need you to pronounce."

"Oh, right." Could I tell her I wasn't catching on? It was midsummer of 1970 and my first night on call. I was the newest intern in a four-hundred-bed community hospital in New Jersey. Everyone here apparently knew what an expiration was. I didn't.

"Doctor?" she said again. It was the voice of a veteran, I could tell. "We've just extubated him, so if you can come up . . ." I didn't want to seem stupid. I was entitled to be called "doctor," even as a first-day intern, but all the rungs of the system rose above me.

"I'll be right there," I said and headed for the wards. Just a year before, I had graduated from medical school in India. Six months of that year were spent in a village posting where the lights went out every time it rained. I had not actually set foot in an American hospital until I became a doctor in one. So far, all I knew about America came from watching two hours of color TV in my hotel room the night before. The hospital had wired me a plane ticket from New Delhi and cab fare to the hotel. I was supposed to rest awhile and then report for duty. All of this I learned long distance, but it was enough. I was very eager to train in advanced American medicine.

My wife, Rita, and I had never seen a color TV before. On the screen, two bodies were being wheeled into an emergency room after a police chase. We could see bullet wounds and blood. I was amazed. "Rita," I said suddenly, "those men they shot, they're taking them to *my* hospital!" What if I had arrived a day earlier? I went to sleep thinking about it.

Now it was the next night, and I was more than a little nervous about being on call alone. I was supposed to handle all the emergencies for the hospital and admit patients I deemed serious enough to need a bed. I was told not to wake up my chief resident unless the situation became impossible to handle alone. I was determined not to let that happen. They could shoot whom they wanted to. I waited. After two hours, the time began to drag, so I went to the cafeteria and bolted a sandwich. When I came back, the nurses said I hadn't missed anything. I waited some more. At about eight the first call came. Surgical Four was having its expiration. There's no limit to what they have in America, I thought.

When I stepped onto the ward floor, the first thing I saw was a small crowd, about eight people, gathered outside one of the rooms. A nurse softly padded over and whispered, "The expiration is in 441, Doctor. I'll come with you." She parted a way and led me into the darkened room. A certain unmistakable tone came from the visitors as I walked through, but I didn't know exactly what I would see. The nurse had sounded routine, a little subdued. What attitude was I supposed to wear? Without warning, my heart started pounding. *Real medicine. Real doctor.*

So that's what one looked like here. Surrounded by dangling IV tubes, oxygen tanks, a heart monitor, a respirator, and more metering gadgetry that I was as yet unfamiliar with, on a stark bed stripped of covers lay a man. He must have been about fifty-five. His frame was wasted and his skin looked yellowish. His bulging eyes stared at the ceiling without a blink. He was so still. His caved-in chest showed no sign of rising and falling. I glanced at the monitor. Nothing. My pulse went racing suddenly into my temples, and the floor sagged a few inches.

"Is he *dead?*" I blurted out.

"I told you we had an expiration." The nurse searched me with a glance. A few seconds went by. "Why don't you pronounce him?" she asked. "I have to get back to my station. Break's in twenty minutes."

A mortal body that has been discarded a minute before is not at all like a cadaver. If I wanted to press my palm against this human husk, it would feel just slightly cool, but it would get colder and colder as long as I held on. I had no notion of doing such a thing. Strangeness can be very close to dread. When I was five, my grandfather died of heart failure in the house one night. I was asleep. My grandmother bundled me out as quickly as she could so that I would not be frightened when the women of our house started wailing. I think I must have heard a little, anyway, or perhaps I confused it with the look on her face.

"What am I supposed to do?" I asked timidly.

"Say he's dead," the nurse told me. She waited a second. "Only a doctor can do that over here." She added a note of emphasis when she said "over here," but she didn't mean it personally. During the Vietnam doctor shortage, the hospital had scraped up five Germans and two Indians to be the staff physicians. At least the Indians spoke English.

I looked at the screens. Everything flat. I was like the last machine, the one that said the others were right. "Sure, he's dead."

"Then you're supposed to tell the family," she said. "That's all of them, out there."

We walked out to face the eight strangers huddled together in the corridor. They looked at me with that prepared look. The nurse nudged me from behind. I took my stethoscope out of my jacket and hung it around my neck. Oh God, I had forgotten to ask what the dead man's name was. One of the men came forward.

"Doctor —"

I was trembling faintly inside, but I cut him short.

"I'm sorry to have to tell you this, sir," I said, "but we have had an expiration." Two of the women burst into tears and took comfort in each other's arms. Another of the men popped up and said in a businesslike way, "I'll get the funeral home." He trotted off toward the phones.

I was staring at the floor, not wanting to say a word more but feeling that I should. The nurse tugged at my arm. She had a decent heart. "Come on, Doctor, we keep the coffee behind the station. Want some? The cigarette machine is over there." I looked gratefully at her. She seemed wonderfully neutral just at that moment. Without any comment or bother, her expression simply said, You look like you could use something.

My first American patient had been a dead man. It wasn't much as I had expected, and not just the corpse. Everything had been medically proper, yet so unhealthy. The machines were in the room and the family was outside the door. That seemed peculiar to me. In India, the family is in the room and the machines are nowhere. I followed the nurse.

After a few hours, my shift became more and more hectic, but the rest of the night seemed not so bad. I worked hard for the next ten hours. I didn't drink one cup of coffee to keep me going but five, and I smoked not one cigarette but a pack. I treated a middle-aged man for an overdose of barbiturates, a young woman with severe bleeding after she attempted to perform an abortion on herself, a vagrant drunk with several long lacerations to the scalp, and a retired lawyer in the throes of a massive heart attack. When the night was over and my shift on call came to its end, I almost felt like a hero. I had saved all these people. My chief resident congratulated me. He was happy that no one had waked him all night for once. He took me to breakfast in the cafeteria, and I dragged on the last couple of cigarettes and cups of coffee while I made my full report. He was encouraging.

"Keep it up and you'll get out of here with a good recommendation. You want to make it to Boston or someplace like that?" I nodded. "Really, you've got a chance, the big league is not so far away." I took his word for it. He was serious and imposing, a fat resident in his third year. Now that he was chief resident, he was used to being right. He said good-bye and told me to get some rest: I was on call again in twelve hours.

I went over to the dormitory where interns rested between shifts. I placed my clothes over the back of a chair and lay down on a cot, but I was too exhausted to sleep. Part of me went racing ahead, wanting nothing more than to get back into the ER and handle more patients. Another part kept touching a sore spot. The whole episode with my first patient couldn't have lasted more that five minutes, seven at most, but I was nagged by a sense of failure. The restless emotions I felt then I can easily feel to this day. I blamed myself for not bringing solace to a dying man, yet we had no relation to each other at all. I had not even drawn a sheet over him or held him for a moment in my thoughts. All at once, but for good, I saw the great abnormality of my world.

I came to medicine when I was sixteen. On the day I graduated from high school, I surprised my father by saying, "Daddy, I want to be a doctor" — blessed words in India when you are the eldest son and your father is a physician. He was overjoyed that, after years of indifference toward medicine, I wanted to be like him. Since boyhood I had been madly in love with soccer and cricket, and whenever I thought for a moment about my future, I saw myself probably as a journalist. Now I decided that medicine was the right pursuit for me, and my motivation grew the more I dwelt on it. I wanted to heal people and make them happy, I was sure of it.

I had been suddenly converted to medicine by reading Sinclair Lewis's novel *Arrowsmith*. My father had seen patients every day of my life, of course, but they had not registered on me. It took a book. I can't remember much about Arrowsmith himself, except that he was a heroic researcher, a microbe hunter driven by a dedication so incredible that it is painful now to recall it literally:

"God give me unclouded eyes and freedom from haste. God give me quiet and relentless anger against all pretense and all pretentious work and all work left slack and unfinished. God give me a restlessness whereby I may neither sleep nor accept praise till my observed results equal my calculated results or in pious glee I discover and assault my error. God give me strength not to trust to God!"

These words once thrilled me. I can hardly read them now, but I am glad that at that age I swallowed the story whole. It had what I needed — the hero was a doctor and the doctor was a hero. At moments he was almost a god, bringing healing to skeptical mortals like an angelic doctor. Arrowsmith spoke words that were more than words. They were sparks hammered hot from the anvil of his dedication. I embraced his dedication and his life, and I would go forth like him.

While I was going through this, I don't believe I mentioned the book to my father. He must have considered, however, that I might be motivated by fantasy. He told me soberly about the burden of work I was taking on to become a doctor. Until then I had shown no interest in medicine, so my background in science was sketchy. He quickly filled my nights at home with tutors in math and chemistry, hired for his lagging but determined boy. The boy was ready to study now and burning to get ahead. My father, so immensely pleased, only repeated his cautions and tried to make me see that doctoring was not so idealistic as I thought.

I lay there in my dorm room that night thinking about it. In the end, after six years of studying, medicine was turning out to have too little to do with healing and making people happy. It had to do instead with my work in the hospital, treating strangers for injuries and maladies that had dropped into their lives, pronouncing a few of them, the most unlucky ones, as expirations. I thought about myself a lot before I forced myself to sleep, but, on reflection, I didn't think about my patients much. We had all met and parted in a few moments. It would have been hard to look at them directly. The girl in desperate agony from her abortion was probably no better off now, even if she wasn't bleeding anymore. The drunk reeled around the ER, out of his senses, oblivious to the streaming gash across his forehead. The gray-faced lawyer clutched at his chest, certain that at that very moment he was dying. The ashamed man with the barbiturate overdose — he was probably a respectable addict who had taken one too many that night, or maybe two. Maybe a lot more than two. I didn't know any of their names. I was thinking of them, if I thought about them at all, as the abortion, the overdose, the laceration, and the heart attack. They were my America.

In a way, it was beginning to seem normal. The veterans had grown used to it. I wasn't going to let it get to me, either. I could already see 1971 as the year I bagged a residency at a teaching hospital in Boston. I lay there dreaming of Harvard as much as anything else. The boy in me still burned to get ahead. I had been told that the ticket out was a good recommendation from the chief of medicine at this hospital. I could do what it took. I was making a good impression from day one. It was easy for me to mix with the nurses at their station, who sloughed off their boredom with jokes and coffee in between ambulances. When an ambulance did drive up, the scene changed in an instant, almost to hysteria. We *moved*.

I lived for that action, and I knew I would be good at it. But for one night I was more a stranger than anything else. Who were these people? How was my life connected with theirs? At some point I dozed off and then clicked awake with a feeling in my stomach that wouldn't be denied. I made it to the bathroom in time and vomited up ham and eggs, coffee, and nicotine. We didn't ingest such things at home. I lay down again, feeling wobbly and cold. Maybe I didn't need a residency at Harvard that much. My first patient was slipping into a shallow grave, and I was marching on. I had meters to read. After a few minutes of these night thoughts, I slept like a stone.

But medicine *should* be about healing people and making them happy. I have had a great deal more time to think about that. Medicine began as more than either science or art. Hippocrates, who walks with every physician, really was an angelic doctor. He claimed descent directly from Aesculapius, the Greek god of healing. In his own lifetime he was revered. He did not just sew up wounds; he added a stitch toward his patient's immortality. We do not know much about the methods of Hippocrates, but we have some of his words. His medicine was wisdom. In fragments of his teaching we can read such statements as this: "Even though a patient may be aware that his condition is perilous, he may yet recover because he has faith in the goodness of his physician." In taking the Hippocratic Oath itself, every doctor swears to this: "I will keep pure and holy both my life and my art."

Since we know very little about the practice of the art Hippocrates was master of, his noble words do not have much connection to reality anymore. The medicine I was taught had been stripped of ideals altogether in favor of a practical zeal for repairing the bodies of sick people. The best doctors I have met in every field are scientists of great integrity and skill. Their goal in life is to track down the cause of disease with precise objectivity and then, they hope, to wipe it out. I can state without even pausing to think about it that no colleague of mine has ever alluded to his pure and holy art.

For their part, the ancients appeared to have little in the way of a scientific foundation for their medicine, but they grasped the nature of man. Their first principle was that health requires a balance within the body. As a piece of received truth, this is easy enough to roll off the tongue, but its implications have been carried far from the ancient world. Today we speak of the body's homeostatic mechanisms, and we pursue biochemical research to discover such things as how the autonomic nervous system mediates the secretions of the endocrine glands. But we are still talking about balance within the body, and we still find it absolutely vital to preserve it.

The ancients also believed that man's inner nature mirrors nature as we observe it around us. Cosmos, or the universe, comprised two fundamental and related realms, the inner and outer. Balancing their forces made it possible for life to continue in harmony. The two ran on parallel tracks, so to speak, and throwing either one into imbalance spelled disaster for both.

The ancient physicians thought they understood the universal basis of life, and they desired to live from its source. Their precepts for health may sound simple-minded to us now because they are not based on reliable information about the body. The Greeks had either bad data about physiology or no data at all. It is therefore hard to credit their view of medicine. Accurate information seems after all so much more *real* than wisdom.

Hippocrates knew nothing about so elementary a fact as the circulation of the blood. He thought of blood as a pure vehicle for the elements of creation — earth, air, fire, and water — and he held that the purest blood must reside nearest the heart, the seat of the purest affections. He and his contemporaries argued whether consciousness could be located in the brain or the bloodstream. Choosing one or the other put you into entirely different camps of Greek medicine.

This seems like a ridiculously primitive disagreement, but the ancient physicians collectively held on to some invaluable assumptions that no one debated. They assumed that man and the entire world were endowed with life, intelligence, and a soul. Since they believed that every bit of the living world contributed to human well-being for better or worse, the ancients built their centers of medicine at sites of great beauty and sanctity. A hospital was very much like a temple. Patients came for inner as well as outer restoration, and their physicians found the fresh air and sunlight to be highly beneficial for both. In his counsel to doctors, Hippocrates wrote one great dictum: "Nature is the curer of sickness." His famed center of medicine on the island of Kos was reputed to contain six thousand medicinal plants, but he knew stronger remedies than any of them: "Leave your drugs in the pot at the pharmacy if you cannot cure the patient with food."

His complete trust in Nature sounds radical now. But if he turned out to be right, wouldn't we all feel nothing less than immense relief? The ancients proposed that nature, meaning our own inner nature, had sufficient means to keep us completely healthy. Their ideal was a state of health that harbored no thoughts of sickness at all. (I am reminded of the old custom in India whereby a physician was paid only if everyone in his village was well. Even if he could cure them, cases of disease were charged to the doctor's neglect.) In other words, health was like freedom. A free life did not confine itself to boundaries and precautions. It was lived spontaneously, taking its nourishment from air, sun, food, and philosophy, and the more spontaneous it could be, the stronger it stood.

Nothing in our medical system comes close to this sort of inspiration. In exchange for ideal health, we accept a view that is more practical and (so we say) more rational. Our science attempts to understand the body one piece at a time, in terms of cells, tissues, and organs. It protects our health the same way, one disease at a time.

But a rational system can wander so far from the source of its inspiration that it turns back on itself. I recently had lunch with the dean of social medicine at a prestigious medical school. We had not met before, and this talk was at my request. I was proposing to him that a conference be held at his school on the medicines of the East, which are the last repositories for the old ideal of man in harmony with Nature. The dean is a physician, an expert in diseases on the larger social scale, including the Far East, but he was skeptical about what I proposed. He adamantly declared that he could not understand why anyone praised Eastern medicine, whose concepts were utterly mumbo-jumbo as far as he could tell.

"I've heard from Eastern doctors, and their heads are filled with mystical ideas. We won't have to listen to all this mystical rubbish, will we?" he complained. That I was from India and might have a personal stake in such ideas didn't phase him.

"The belief that man and Nature are bound up together in one body is part of these systems," I said, a bit coolly. "It's not some kind of mystical nonsense. They have found therapies that work as well as ours. It's just a different basic concept. Our medicine is based on a concept, too, as you know."

He snorted.

I will not be forced to invent that he was a fat man in a pin-striped suit smoking a cigar, because he actually was all of that. He also made the memorable remark, "For God's sake, if you do hold this conference, don't let me hear from those *holistic* health people. I've got enough trouble from them already." The dean glared down at his luncheon plate, probably thinking about the holistic menace. No one who really believed in the medicine he practices could be that aggressively closed-minded.

After we parted, I became angry that his attitude had forced me to act like an enemy to real medicine. His sort of real medicine has its glaring faults, though not mystical ones. It is not news that confidence in doctors is becoming rare. The incredible expense and complexity of the present system is known to everybody.

What is less well known, because doctors do not discuss it very openly, is the futility of practicing medicine without a basic ideal. What kind of holistic rubbish would the dean have found in these two lines:

> Rejoice at your inner powers, for they are the makers of wholeness and holiness in you,
> Rejoice at seeing the light of day, for seeing makes truth and beauty possible.

They happen to come from Hippocrates, and as long as they have meaning, medicine is saved from becoming soulless.

I was probably lucky to go through a dark night in New Jersey. In a moment of insecurity, I felt that not the physician but the disease had the upper hand. My rational methods, the machines I controlled, and my concepts of treatment seemed to have too little to do with life and too much to do with death. Practicing medicine as we do now makes a doctor's life as nerve-racking as a soldier's. It consists of an endless struggle to conquer disease, and to keep at this, a doctor must deny to himself that disease ultimately wins. If you feel called to practice medicine, these are not the kinds of thoughts you permit yourself. But doctors do face up to them from time to time and wonder what the work is for.

After my troubled night, I became what I was headed for.

I got to be a resident and a specialist. Like the big third-year man who urged me on to Boston, I became a chief resident myself, and so I got used to being right. The dormitories of large teaching hospitals became a second home to me; in time, I had my own practice. Success in the system, however, depended on believing in the system. I used to be much better at that than I am now. My beliefs have been changing very fast, and now I am probably part of the dean's holistic menace. I am amazed at how long it took me to discover something that is almost absurdly simple: a physician must trust in Nature and be happy in himself.

But when you are starting out in New Jersey, it takes time to rejoice at your inner powers.

2

The Mongoose or the Cobra?

POONA, INDIA, 1954. I was seven years old. My mother was away, visiting my grandmother's house, and had taken my four-year-old brother with her. I was home alone after school until my father came in around six o'clock. He looked excited and was beaming.

"Hurry up!" he urged me. "Wash your face, change your clothes, put on a tie. We're going out for some fun."

"Where are we going?" I asked.

"No questions," he insisted. "Wait and see. We're going to have the time of our lives!"

I hopped quickly into a change of clothes, put on my school tie, and hurried out onto the veranda, where my father waited impatiently with his bicycle. I jumped onto the handlebars and off he pedaled through the warm summer night. I had no earthly idea where we were going, but I was thrilled all the same.

My father's legs pumped furiously as we cycled past the Poona bazaars, weaving through the thronging cyclists, rickshaw wallahs, motorbikes, and an occasional car. As we negotiated our way through this area, the Great Poona Cantonment, we saw a small crowd in the square. A snake charmer was blowing skillfully on his flute while before him on the ground a cobra and mongoose circled each other in their killing dance.

"Daddy, stop!" I pleaded. "Can't we watch this?" The two animals are mortal enemies. The mongoose walks round and round the snake, waiting for a chance to leap and bite it on the back of the neck. The cobra rears its head and weaves in the air, knowing that it only has to strike once. The fights are usually short. The mongoose almost always wins.

"No, no," my father said. "We have to hurry or we'll be too late, and then we will wait many lifetimes for another chance like this."

So we sped on. It soon became clear that we were headed for the army barracks. As we got near, my father's pedaling became more furious. We hurried into the compound that housed a small brick building known as the M.I. Room. Everything in the British army constitutes an incident, so sickness and injuries were medical incidents — or M.I. — and this was the facility for them, a sort of combined clinic and dispensary. Officers, common soldiers, and their families all came here with their sore throats, aches and pains, and broken bones. My father worked there, but I had no interest in it at all. The M.I. Room also held a makeshift lecture hall that could seat about seventy-five people when all the miscellaneous dining room chairs were hauled in.

There were already scores of bicycles parked in a jumble outside the M.I. Room when we arrived. My father groaned. The hall was packed to bursting with military doctors and nurses and smelled of starched khaki and crisp white coats, which were everywhere. The air buzzed with excitement, and naturally there was not a seat to be had. What was this all about? I remember being completely at a loss but exhilarated to be with so many grownups. In that charged atmosphere, it was only natural that a little boy should feel especially excited. We waited.

Then applause broke out. People kept clapping harder and

jumping up in front of me. The object of all this clamor turned out to be an old, bespectacled, European-looking gentleman, who slowly approached and mounted the stage. My memory tells me that he had a white beard, but it may be playing tricks, since I outfitted all old, European-looking gentlemen with one. He took the slightest bow of acknowledgment to his ovation, which in time died away. The lights went out, and the hall became very quiet. The European gentleman began to talk and at the same time started projecting pictures on a screen by his side.

I couldn't understand a word he was saying, and all his pictures showed the same thing: lots of white dots with halos around them.

"What's he doing, Daddy?" I piped up.

"Hush, son," was all he could say. "I'll explain it to you later." I mustn't spoil a historic moment in our lives. I tried everything a seven-year-old can do to listen to an old man whose accent he can't comprehend and all of whose pictures, even after half an hour, were of exactly the same thing. I wished we had stopped in the square to see the cobra and mongoose fight. I tugged at Daddy's sleeve and whispered again, but he paid no notice. In a short while I crept away toward the front door and lay down behind it. Before long I was asleep.

When I woke up, it was ten o'clock. The hall was empty. My father was kissing me and exclaiming what a wonderfully well-behaved boy his son was. Now we should be going home. On the way back, the streets were quiet and deserted. My father pedaled home slowly through the dim, narrow lanes, balancing his bicycle with one hand and lighting the way with a flashlight in the other, in the Indian fashion. As we passed through the empty square, I told myself that there was a fresh splash of blood on the ground where the fight had taken place. And I wondered who had won.

We were home very late. My father tucked me into bed

with a gleam in his eyes. He kept me awake one last minute and told me that the European gentleman had been describing the discovery of penicillin.

"In what country is Penicillin?" I wanted to know.

Before he would say any more, my father stood me up on the floor to be sure I was listening and held me straight by the shoulders.

"That man tonight was Fleming, Sir Alexander Fleming. He has discovered a medicine that has already saved hundreds and thousands of lives. Millions more will now be saved because of him. You're one lucky boy to get to hear him tell his story."

Then he gave me a kiss and left the room. In a few minutes I drifted off to sleep for good.

That was my father's brush with greatness in medicine, but to us in the family, he had become great himself. Although a native Indian, he stood on a par with any of the English doctors and had acquired medical training equal to theirs. That was very rare in those days, when Britain was divesting herself of India, the last and largest diamond in the crown of empire.

My father began his climb as a medical officer in the army that fought the Japanese in Burma. Indians were internally divided about helping the British in the Second World War. A certain contingent even took the opportunity to further the cause of Indian independence by opposing the British. My father was not among them. He accepted the traditional marks of prestige conferred upon any Indian who rose in the British ranks and was already the son of an army sergeant. Fighting in Burma was thankless, brutal, and in the end almost futile, since the campaign of "the forgotten army" that struggled there so valorously was overshadowed by the sudden ending of the war when the Americans dropped their atom bombs on Japan.

At one point, however, my father was called away from the front when news came that Lord Mountbatten, the last viceroy of India under King George VI, the last emperor of India, was arriving for a tour of the subcontinent. His medical aide, it turned out, was unavailable, and my father was assigned to that duty on short notice. What it entailed I don't exactly know. My father made it sound as if he stood at attention to hand Lady Mountbatten her aspirin when she arose in the morning. However, the viceroy and his wife were suitably impressed. In a characteristically generous moment, Mountbatten summoned my father as the tour came to its end.

"You've been a good boy," he said. "What do you want out of life?"

My father was confused. "I don't want anything, Your Excellency," he replied.

"You must want something. Come now."

On an impulse, my father said, "I want to train in internal medicine."

Lord Mountbatten immediately issued the orders from which sprang a letter conveying my father to the British military hospital in Poona. My father arrived and presented himself to the medical officer in charge. This man was an eminent Harley Street physician, a cardiologist, who was doing his war service in Poona, inland from the Arabian Sea on the west coast of India, an outpost of empire so far removed that few people there realized his actual importance.

He looked at my father blankly and said, "Who are you? What are you doing here?" Every patient in the hospital, every doctor, and every staff member was white. My father looked conspicuously out of place.

"I'm here to learn medicine," my father replied.

"But that's impossible," the eminent physician said. My father presented the letter from Lord Mountbatten, which he had brought with him. The chief of medicine took one look and said, "All right, show up on rounds tomorrow."

My father rushed back to his quarters and eagerly studied the case histories of the patients who were due to be presented. Grand rounds under the British were morning ceremonies of considerable occasion. Every doctor showed up, and the chief of medicine, presumably dressed in morning coat and cravat, led the procession from ward to ward, quizzing the others on points of difficulty. My father found himself at the very rear. No one spoke to him, no one looked his way. He knew the cases well, but he didn't dare to speak. This silent ritual went on for two months. Moments came up when my father knew an answer when none of the British doctors did, for he studied half the night, day in and day out, to be sure that he would never make a mistake. He held his tongue until it became unbearable, and one day, when even the chief of medicine was stymied, my father blurted out his opinion. As it happened, he was right. The chief of medicine turned to him.

"Who are you?" he asked. "What are you doing here?"

"I've been on grand rounds for two months, sir," my father answered. "I'm studying medicine."

"But that's impossible," the chief said.

My father never went to the hospital without his letter from Mountbatten, and he produced it for the chief. He read it and handed it back without comment, but from that point on, the eminent physician became interested in Krishan Chopra, he called on him, and it became a habit that my father, a tireless worker and dedicated doctor, knew the right answers. When the war ended and the chief was preparing to return to the London Heart Hospital as its director, he called my father in. For the second time, my father heard someone say, "What do you want? Just tell me."

He was just as unprepared as before, but he found himself answering that he wanted to specialize in cardiology. He hardly knew why he said it. His chief saw that my father deserved success and, in time, invited him to come to London. The eminent physician, now a lord, met my father on the docks of Southampton dressed in top hat, frockcoat, and cane. My father delights in recounting that his host apologized for not bringing his wife, but that day she was having lunch with the queen.

The night my father took me to see Fleming, I had such a vivid dream that I can still remember it. I saw thousands of soldiers fallen on a battlefield, all dead. A kindly European man wearing spectacles and a beard was walking among the bodies, spraying them out of a nozzle with teeming little white dots. And as he sprayed them, the men each got up and walked away. Gradually everyone was sprayed, and not a single body remained. But right in the middle of the field lay a black cobra in a pool of its own blood. Its head was smashed and its neck broken. A small mongoose leaped around it in fits and jumps. The European approached and sprayed the snake, but nothing happened. He kept spraying, more and more, until he became frantic, but the cobra still lay in its pool of blood. The mongoose kept dancing its macabre steps.

An obscure dream for a small boy — or is it? I have decided to read it, across the space of thirty years, as a story about medicine and me. The dream concerns a choice. In the bazaar, either the mongoose or the cobra must win, and until the decisive moment, the two circle each other endlessly. The cobra is not necessarily the evil partner in their dance or some hidden deathliness inside me. He also stands for the deepest wisdom and power, and as such, he is revered in India. In many images he can be seen flaring his hood over the throne of a god to protect him. At other times, his erect head is a pedestal for the god to stand on. Now the cobra has been dethroned, however, and when he crept away, he took a world with him. It is no small loss, because some power, perhaps one of great invincibility, was dethroned in us at the same time.

I feel sorry to see the cobra vanish. As he exists in me, I

know he must be more wise than dangerous. And yet my very fear of him makes me glad that there is a mongoose, always circling, always watching, ready to defend me. Medicine in the scientific mold is all mongoose and no cobra. All that is wise and instinctive has been banished in favor of constant vigilance and the mongoose-like hunt for its prey; only the medical researcher is stalking diseases and cures, diseases and cures. It is very hard for most people to see why there should be any cobra to it at all. This is because we do not really want to accept Nature as a whole. We have exiled from it those parts that we fear. Only then we must pay the price of endlessly defending ourselves in case a new fear, a new disease, returns. How long can we stand the strain?

The East is not necessarily better off than the West in this regard. After two centuries of British rule, a very Western idea of Nature inevitably soaked through Indian life. Very few of us realize the stupendous view of human potential that is India's bequest to humanity. Indians may hear the old words in temples or read them in books, but we do not find practicality in them, or in the ways they fostered. To give an example: when I was a child, I knew dimly that there was medicine different from the kind my father practiced. It was the traditional Indian medicine called Ayurveda, from the two Sanskrit words *ayus*, or "life," and *veda*, or "knowledge."

This "knowledge of life" comes from origins as sacred as those that fathered Hippocrates, but they are far older. According to the beginning of the *Charaka Samhita*, which is considered a definitive source, Ayurveda came as a gift to mankind from the immortals. In some ancestral era, the people of India had fallen prey to sickness and spiritual ignorance. Seven of the greatest rishis, or seers, took pity on them and decided to ask help from the gods. They sat together in a circle, meditating deeply, and summoned Indra, who is the manifestation of everything in creation. One of the rishis, Bharadwaja, sat outside the circle to receive Indra's complete knowledge about life, not just man's but the lives of animals and plants, stones and atoms, and indeed everything that could be said to have a life span in the plan of creation. This knowledge, encompassing time from the smallest part of a split second to the age of the cosmos, was Ayurveda.

The rishis gave it to the people, to be applied to themselves and saved forever. Thus Ayurveda signifies more than a system of medicine. It is India's guide to life. Rabindranath Tagore, the great Bengali writer, touched upon this tradition in a passage devoted to the true Indian view of the world: "For us, the highest purpose of the world is not merely living in it, knowing it and making use of it, but realizing our own selves in it through expansion of sympathy, comprehending and uniting ourselves with it in perfect union."

At the soul of India there is an expansive spiritual joy. Ayurveda is completely a part of this view, and therefore its aim is the constant expansion of man's happiness. Even when I was ignorant of any good that might come from Ayurveda and completely captivated by the West, I knew a famous verse from the Ayurvedic texts that declared, "Ayurveda is for immortality." In another place, the texts say, "The inner intelligence of the body is the ultimate and supreme genius. It mirrors the wisdom of the universe." Because Ayurveda springs from deep sources, it has outlasted India's sad decline. To this day it constitutes 70 percent of health care in the country, but principally in the rural areas, where the poor cannot be reached by our new and enlightened medicine.

Words that reach out to the stars and a soul filled with joy. India did not show me these for a very long time. It is much easier to see the signs of failure instead. Any visitor to India will of course find its people on the whole "underdeveloped," in the sense that they are poor and have few machines. The water is tainted, the food looks suspicious, and don't even think about the telephones! India looks on the surface like a land apart, fixed in its past. But the essential change under the skin has occurred, silently and almost with gratitude. The cobra is dead.

In our family, the idea of resorting to traditional Ayurveda, with its thousands of unproven herbs and even more of its pointless rituals, was heresy. My father proudly practiced Western medicine and looked on his accomplishments as a personal triumph. He had every reason to think that modern India would be well off without the ignorant old ways. Ayurveda, being "unscientific" to Western eyes, could join the other castoffs. It never occurred to me or to my father that Ayurveda might be something great. That we might find a teacher who could revive Ayurveda for us did not so much as cross our minds. We did not pierce through to the heart of its essential truth, that man must live in the stream of Nature and balance his life as Nature demands. "Nature is the curer of illness" — all healing in the ancient world, from Greece to India to China, derived from this precept, but Ayurveda goes on to restore man as a lord of life:

> As is the atom, so is the universe,
> As is the microcosm, so is the macrocosm.
>
> As is the human body, so is the cosmic body,
> As is the human mind, so is the cosmic mind.

This is a hard thing to come to terms with. Very few of us really know how to grasp an ideal. Our worst fear is that we will one day encounter our own genius. For us, there is no longer a great dance between cobra and man in which man can be fearless. To be really fearless, man would have to be on a par with Indra, the wholeness of creation. But in his mind Nature has set him apart. The shock of being thrown out of the dance is still upon us, but we don't allude to it. Man has made himself a half-god in a world where perfect godliness is forbidden.

I think certain of the women in our immediate household, and certainly all the older generation, gave credence to the time-honored precepts of Ayurveda, but to my father they were rubbish. The old precepts, I should say at once, were not peculiar. Ayurveda mandates cleanliness and hygiene, pure food and water, and balanced nutrition, but not in the language of objective science. A turning point in my father's life had come when he left his family to go to Britain for advanced medical training as a cardiologist, placing his young wife and children in the care of his father. The old man, my grandfather, had developed a severe heart condition. For relief, he turned to the herbs and practices of Ayurveda. When my father heard of this, he was perturbed. He demanded that my grandfather abandon this nonsense and call in a Western-style heart specialist. It was ludicrous and humiliating that the son should be training as a cardiologist while the father went to native doctors. I am too far removed now to know if my grandfather was sustained by his trust in the Ayurvedic physicians and if that helped his condition. I do know that he called in the heart specialist, dutifully took the prescribed drugs, and died two weeks later.

My father took this as a terrible blow. He immediately returned to us in India, accepted a teaching position, and forgot his life in the great medical centers of London. If anybody thought that Grandfather had been doing better under the care of Ayurveda than under the heart specialist, we never whispered it to my father. Nor could it have occurred to anyone of his generation that there might be a marriage between Ayurveda and modern scientific medicine. Why should anyone wake up the cobra? My father was being shaped by circumstances that were sweeping India to liberation and promising a modern life for at least a small part of the population. As with me when I went to America, his success in the system depended on his belief in the system.

As my father's son, I was an unlikely person to rediscover Ayurveda for myself. It required the intervention of a new force in my life. When that arrived, which is a later part of

this story, the appeal of Ayurvedic wisdom became self-evi-
dent, and the idea of a medicine that keeps man whole was
tremendously welcome. I found that I wanted to rejoin the
dance after all. But it took something like a change in my
world view.

Ralph Waldo Emerson wrote a thrilling aphorism to describe this change: "When half-gods go, the gods arrive." Until
that undreamt-of time, the cobra and the mongoose, the
mongoose and the cobra, keep circling without peace, certain
of their mutual hostility.

3

Junk Heaps at the Castle of Death

WHAT I REMEMBER of Jabalpur when I was ten: its very
drab military cantonment, which was Daddy's new medical
posting. Groves of mango and guava trees, right next to the
house, where we could play until the evening shadows turned
us out. The congestion of the railway lines, riders starting out
from every place and ending up in our lap. And a new breed
of people whose manners placed them outside our family laws
forever.

These new people were the Anglo-Indians. No one fully
accepted them. The British, who called us "brownies," called
them "khakis." Their fathers were usually English or Irish
soldiers; their mothers were native Indians. I was naturally
too small to consider what lonely women they must have been.
The Anglo-Indian families constituted our respectable poor.
They managed to make their way, but hardly ever into the
ranks of the middle class. The men all seemed to work for the
railways, and they carried themselves, in our eyes, with de-
testable airs. The boys who followed them on the streets would
yell, "Not white, not black, but khaki." Even though I made
friends with some Anglo-Indian boys my own age, I sometimes said this, too, behind their backs.

Most of the Anglo-Indian men were eager to seize any chance to leave home, heading out for Australia or New Zealand. There, someone might accept them, or at least take their British accents for the real thing. As long as they were in Jabalpur, however, the railways gave them plenty of work. The Bombay–to–Calcutta express, chugging for three days across the torrid country, stopped midway in our town. The bogeys were cleaned out — I remember this as the Anglo-Indian word for train buggies — while the stifled passengers descended to wash off two days of grime. The steam engines waited in the yards for their new load of coal. These big, patient black machines always managed in India to look like elephants. Most of the Anglo-Indians could read and write, so it was unthinkable for any to sink as low as the native porters on the trains. They worked instead, in tattered coats and ties, as ticket collectors, engine drivers, and station masters. They scurried about doing paperwork and other clerkly business that added to their self-importance.

Their haughty and educated look fascinated me. I stared openly at their lighter skins and their European clothes. Occasionally I was even permitted to visit the home of an Anglo-Indian school friend for lunch. I would then see things I had never encountered before. The family drank beer with their meals. They ate food that came from tins, unspeakable goods like sausage or, the height of elegance, canned beans. I was offered stewed ox tongue and soup made from pig's feet. Invariably I would politely decline, making the excuse that I was feeling a little sick, which in fact was true.

One day my father announced that my little brother and I were getting an Anglo-Indian nanny named Mrs. Mac-Namara. Her husband, an engine driver, had recently died from a heart attack. She had three children — two sons about our age and a seventeen-year-old daughter. They had no income and no place to go. When my father ran across Mrs. MacNamara as a patient in the army hospital, he felt sorry for her and offered her a job with us. This was a little odd, since we had so far done very well without a nanny all our lives. My mother and grandmother were reluctant at first, but they finally conceded to my father's soft heart.

By this time my father was a lieutenant colonel in the Indian army, in charge of a medical regiment of around six hundred people, other doctors, soldiers, and hospital personnel. He was the least military of commanders, very gentle and soft-spoken in his demeanor, without a trace of military posture beneath his starched uniform. His two outstanding qualities, at work and at home, were his compassion and his absent-mindedness.

The latter quality drove his batman, or personal aide, almost to distraction. This man spent hours polishing my father's shoes, belt buckle, and war medals to a perfect gleam. But then he would have to come rushing into our house once or twice a week to fetch some part of the uniform that my father had forgotten to put on.

If it was his medals, the omission was not important. But in the army there was a ritual connected with relieving an officer of his post that consisted of officially asking him for his belt. Taking that away signified that the reprimanded officer was no longer on duty — and in fact was the same as confining him to house arrest. So on the days when my father walked through the hospital without his belt, having neglected to put it on that morning, the bewildered soldiers thought he was under arrest instead of in command until the batman rushed off frantically to fetch it for the fiftieth time.

Although his official duties as a doctor were confined to the military hospital, my father's skill was greatly respected in the town, too. The civilians held that my father was the sort of physician who could cure anyone. In the middle of the night, after my mother had taken the telephone off the hook, we would hear banging on our door. Opening it a crack, my father would see the worried, pleading face of a city worker, begging the Doctor Sahib to come save his uncle, who was dying. My father always complied with these midnight requests, and over time, I believe many people in Jabalpur felt that having him hold their hands as he sat by the sickbed would be enough to cure them of fever.

He himself believed strongly in such measures (as I do now). My father possessed an absorbing gaze that flowed with compassion. It was a natural attribute — there was not the slightest question of his having to cultivate a bedside manner. And it was not just his patients who received the benefit of his warm, understanding look. When we boys played cricket, it was an all-consuming activity, but I can remember glancing up in the middle of an innings to see my father silently leaning against the fence and watching us.

He had come home to eat lunch, but halfway through the door he would spot us and walk over to observe our game. He never made a sound or attracted attention to himself in any way but would just lean on the fence with half his medals missing from his tunic. His gentle brown eyes are there looking at me whenever I think back, as much as the new cricket bats that he would occasionally (and just as silently) leave by the fence from time to time. On many of these days he got no lunch at all when he realized that his hour was up and he had to be back in the wards.

So it was no surprise to my mother that he had taken pity on Mrs. MacNamara. The only demand set down was that no ox tongues or roast beef should be cooked in our kitchen, and the "nanny," having practically nothing to do for two boys aged seven and ten, was expected to help with the everyday cooking and washing. Our large colonial house had been originally outfitted with separate servants' quarters, now known as the annex. In a little while, Mrs. MacNamara and her children moved in.

The new boys, Terence and Philip, were gratefully included in the games I played with my brother. We were too used to being just the two of us, chasing each other through the mango trees. Now that we were four, we immediately formed a cricket club. There was already a decent cricket pitch at the back of our compound. In a few days we were spending half of our time there and the other half at the annex. Everything was different where they lived, especially the smells.

It was not long before Mrs. MacNamara surprised us by acquiring a boyfriend. His name was Mr. De Cruz, and he was an Anglo-Indian who had no job or evident means of support. He had only Mrs. MacNamara. Orthodox Indian families, even when Westernized, as we were, did not know of such a thing. My mother and grandmother turned distrustful and unhappy. My father did not consider the issue worth discussing. But my brother, Sanjiv, and I became completely enraptured with this man, whom we all called Uncle.

First of all, Uncle was a great artist. He could sketch pictures of people that looked just like them. He made a specialty of tinting black-and-white photographs, the only kind we ever saw, until they looked like paintings. He did this with portrait photos of my mother and grandmother, who all at once began to look upon Uncle with a measure of kindliness and tolerance. He could also play the violin very beautifully. But most of all Uncle was a great storyteller. He would sit every evening with a glass of bad sweet sherry in his hand and tell us endless adventures that he solemnly declared to be true. Tiger hunts in the Nilgiri forest, ghosts who scared people to death, and Uncle's own war exploits on the frontier of Germany were his favorite ones. He also read to us from adult books and explained the difficult parts as he went along. I wish I could remember how he explained Huxley's *Brave New World* and Orwell's *1984* to us. I only remember that he did it with special conviction.

Uncle could fix anything and knew everything there was to know. He helped us cure our new cricket bats with linseed oil. (I cannot even think of this ritual today without seeing him as part of it.) He never lacked the time to shout advice to us while we played our afternoon innings or to find larger and bloodier tigers for his tales. This entirely wonderful person sometimes disappeared, however, for long stretches of time. No one seemed to know exactly where he went or when he would return. Later, we discovered that Uncle was helping to organize the Communist Party of India. After one of these trips, when we had an inkling of his business, we asked him what a Communist was. He said that a Communist was someone who believed in equality. One day I asked if Uncle himself was a Communist.

"I am a Communist and an atheist," he replied. This did not bother us at all until Uncle explained that an atheist was someone who did not believe in God. We were shocked. Not believe in God? We rushed to tell Mother and Grandmother all about it, and from that point on Uncle's lovely pictures did him no good whatever. My mother said at supper that it should be politely hinted to Mrs. MacNamara that she find another position. My grandmother was more direct.

"Throw them out," she said. "He's a devil."

For a while we were forbidden to visit Uncle again. We were consigned to afternoons with Grandmother, whose stories of Rama and Krishna came from the Scriptures. They were not at all disappointing, though. They had great magic, adventure, and mystery in them — magic, mystery, and adventure that was also devout. The moral tags were easy to understand and stuck for life. More astonishing, Grandmother implied that the most awesome of powers did not belong to just gods and *sidhas,* the perfected beings. They were in us, too, only we were not yet perfected. Could a boy really fly through the air or read people's minds or cure mortals of horrible diseases simply by touching them? My grandmother stood firm. The *sidhas* in the Vedas could do all this and more. One day we would become like them. She never told us what it took to become perfected. Apparently it was more than merely growing up, since she herself, an absolute believer, could not fly, even if we asked her all day.

One of her stories especially impressed Sanjiv. It derived, like almost all of hers, from the *Ramayana*, the epic story of Lord Rama. It is very common for tales of Rama to be extracted and simplified for children; even the comic books in India are likely to show not Superman flying through the air, but Hanuman the monkey-king, fetching a mountain from the Himalayas so that Lord Rama might have one herb that grew on its slopes.

The story that impressed Sanjiv has to do with brotherly devotion. Through an intrigue involving two rival wives of the king, Rama's father, it has been decreed that Rama be banished to wander in the forest for fourteen years. He is to go only with his bride, Sita, but his younger brother, Lakshman, is so loyal that he vows to accompany Rama into exile, no matter what may befall them. The three, Rama, Sita, and Lakshman, have many adventures in the jungle, but the crowning one is this. As they are out hunting one day, they see a deer leap past them. The animal is of such surpassing beauty that Sita, who has some of the unflattering attributes of a spoiled princess, begs to have its skin as a present.

Rama agrees to go hunting for the animal immediately. He departs from their hut, leaving Lakshman behind to guard his wife and telling him under no circumstances to abandon her. After some time passes, Rama has not returned. Sita begins to fret, and after several days with no sign of him, she becomes frantic. She begs Lakshman to go in search of Rama, but the brother refuses. Under no condition will he break a pledge he has made to his elder brother.

When she hears this, Sita becomes angry. She accuses Lakshman of not loving Rama enough to go save him. Worse than this, she implies that Lakshman might be reluctant to leave because he has his own interests in her. Now Lakshman is in torment, torn between his sworn duty and his deep love for Rama. He decides finally upon a solution. Being possessed of great powers, or *sidhis*, he draws a magic line around the hut. He adjures Sita not to cross this line on any account and says that any man or demon who attempts to cross it will be instantly consumed in flames, no matter how potent his own magic is.

Saying this, Lakshman slings his bow over his shoulder and departs. Sita obeys his orders until a holy man, a wandering monk, appears outside the hut, begging for alms. In India, hospitality to a guest is a sacred duty. Sita is tempted to cross the line, knowing that no harm can come to her from a monk. And the monk shows no desire to cross the line anyway, since he has taken a vow of chastity. So she asks him to stand at a distance while she walks across the line to place alms in his bowl. As soon as she does this, the monk instantly transforms himself into his true shape — Ravana, king of the demons himself — and with one swoop he seizes her as his prize.

This one episode from the narrative, which goes on for many thousands of lines, made Sanjiv realize the utmost importance of obeying the Rama in his life — me. I found his devotion very useful soon thereafter.

Both Sanjiv and I were thrilled when my father returned from London one year with an air rifle as our present, what Americans call a BB gun. Although my grandmother did not approve of it, on the grounds that we were sure to shoot ourselves, the gun became the main prop in all our games.

One day Sanjiv was shooting target practice against a post. I moved behind the post, and he asked me to go away. But in school the Christian brothers had just taught us about William Tell. I told Sanjiv that we should play that game. Even at seven he was a good enough marksman to hit the post without touching me. Reluctantly he fired. Unfortunately he missed the post: the BB hit me right on the point of my chin, and blood began to flow.

Sanjiv was terribly upset, and although I tried to reassure

him that I was not badly hurt, it took a great deal of persuasion to keep him from running back to the house immediately. Finally, I reminded him that I was Rama and he Lakshman. Out of sacred devotion he had to obey my orders, and my orders were not to tell our parents what had happened. At this, his eyes grew big and he promised.

When my father came home that evening, we told him that my wound was from a point of barbed wire I had fallen on while climbing over the fence. He accepted this explanation and applied an antiseptic. That would have been the end of the incident, except that the wound refused to heal. Days passed, and still the spot looked red and swollen, no matter what medicines my father gave me, including injections of antibiotic.

My grandmother could stand it no longer. She took me aside and began to rub my chin with turmeric, a common kitchen spice that was one of the Ayurvedic remedies she knew. As she was applying it, she felt a tiny bump and said that something was lodged in my chin. My father couldn't find anything, but Grandmother wouldn't relent, insisting that I be taken to the army hospital for X-rays. My father gave in, the pictures were taken, and he was amazed to see that a BB had worked its way deep under the skin.

When Sanjiv and I were interrogated again, the strain was too much for him. He broke his oath and confessed what had really happened. I'm sure this did him a great deal of good, since he had been moping guiltily for almost a week. My grandmother's stock rose enormously. Before, my father had paid grudging respect whenever she bypassed his medicine to prescribe a little ginger for a cold or some turmeric paste for a sore, because these remedies had an annoying habit of working perfectly. Now he actually began to refer some of his more difficult cases to her at mealtimes. No one outside the family knew that the great doctor respected his mother as a higher authority, but he had to admit that more than once her Ayurvedic notions helped his patients.

During the time of his banishment, my grandmother did not have to remind me to avoid Uncle. My guilt had made me afraid of him, and I did not want to meet his glance if I could help it. One day, however, I walked past the annex and saw him on the veranda. He was seated before his easel, ready to paint the sunset.

"Where have you been?" he asked me casually. "I've missed you. You've missed some real stories, you know."

"I've been busy," I muttered.

"Oh my," Uncle said in his comic voice. "The boy is grown."

As I looked at him, I relaxed. I loved Uncle. The idea that he was a Communist and an atheist frightened me, but he was otherwise so wonderful. I walked onto the veranda.

"You were joking about being a Communist, weren't you?" I asked. By this time the Christian missionaries who ran our school had informed us of the absolute evil represented by Communists. They called them "Reds" in a manner that left no doubt about blood and ruin.

"Not at all," Uncle coolly answered. "I am a Communist, and there's nothing wrong about it. We are people who simply feel that everybody should be equal. That's a good thing, isn't it? Come on, look at me."

I must have looked at him. He was wonderful to me. It was ridiculous to think of him as a Red. "But you're also an atheist, Uncle." I had to say it. "You don't believe in God."

Uncle put down his brushes and came over to me.

"Don't you want to learn to think for yourself?" he said. "I don't believe in God. I'm not saying you have to listen to me or agree with my opinion. You don't. But you don't have to listen to those idiots at school. Do you believe everything your grandmother says?"

His logic held such a guilty appeal. Thank God no one was around to hear him.

"Then what happens when a man dies?" I asked. "Where do we go?"

"Nowhere. We just cease to be. We are extinct." Uncle

sounded very decisive. I remember his words, spoken precisely like snips of the scissors. He was cutting something. "Life doesn't go anywhere when you die, it's just gone."

"But where?"

Around the corner, in the yard next to the annex, was an abandoned jalopy. Uncle had the inspiration to point it out to me. It was barely recognizable after a few monsoons, just a junk heap.

"That was once alive, too," he said. "It could move. Its engine was the life in that car. But now it doesn't do anything. The wires are rotted out and the battery is dead. It's rust. The life hasn't gone anywhere, has it? It just isn't there anymore."

Snip, snip, snip. He was cutting — a thread.

"Pretty soon, you won't even see this. The weather will keep on working, the rust will crumble some more. If you come back here in ten years, this car won't even exist anymore. It will just go pooh! and turn to dust."

I remembered my grandfather the day he took us all to the cinema to see *Ali Baba and the Forty Thieves*. We had just gotten news from England that my father had been elected to the Royal College of Physicians. Everyone came to our house to receive sweets directly from my grandfather's hand. He all but danced around us in his jubilation. Now he was extinct? I pulled away from Uncle and went back to the house. Uncle was always right. I sat in my room and thought of Grandfather going pooh! in Uncle's dramatic way. I felt very hurt. I felt strangely free.

The thread of innocence is probably not snipped all at once. It is a gradual process that takes years. But terrible moments do stand out in that process, like seismic cracks appearing as an indication that the earth has shifted dangerously. At every stage of losing innocence, something shifts, too, and cracks appear. The result was judged by Emerson in a sentence from his essay *Nature:* "The reason why the world lacks unity, and lies broken and in heaps, is because man is disunited within himself."

Such a clear insight, coming like a bolt of sanity, does not occur to ordinary people, but everyone, I am sure, can identify with it. The traits of trust, simple belief, and devotion are usually left behind somewhere in every childhood. They are not easy to recapture, because they require innocence. Bringing the broken world back together is as delicate as repairing a torn spiderweb.

Most people are not sensitive to this because they have lived for so long amid heaps and ruins. These are just poetic terms for experience and its troubles. We live with them as a normal part of being complex adults. To become experienced is all but synonymous with becoming mature. When Uncle held out the full-blown flower of his skepticism to me, I believe he thought he was doing me some good.

There is no doubt that he was describing reality, as he and most people now see it. But innocence may rule a reality just as convincing, if it can be regained. I do not mean trying to become a child again, but placing innocence on a higher plane. To illustrate this, here is another tale in my grandmother's style, which speaks of innocence as the requirement for immortality. I imagine that all Indian children know it, about the little boy who humbled Death. The little boy was named Nachiketas, which means, roughly, "not possessing knowledge." It implies a wisdom born of innocence. To me, his story came directly from Grandmother, but actually it comes from one of the greatest Upanishads, which are considered by Indian sages to unfold the essence of human wisdom. We children just took Nachiketas to be a boy who was much braver than we were, so of course we liked him immediately.

In the beginning of the tale, a man greedy for everlasting blessings had reached the age where he must give away his property to the priests and retreat to the forest to gain under-

standing. This was the third stage of life in the traditional
Vedic culture of India. After passing the stages of childhood
studies and raising a family, a man knew that he should seek
spiritual attainment when his eldest son reached up to his
shoulder. This man, Vajasravasa, had come to that stage. He
called together the priests to distribute his personal wealth.
But his son, Nachiketas, noticed that his father had chosen
to give away only the cows that were barren and gave no
milk or that were too lame even to walk. He saw that his
father could achieve nothing worthwhile if he began like this,
so he asked him a question.

"Father," Nachiketas inquired, "I am your most valuable
possession. To whom are you going to give me?"

Vajasravasa said nothing. His son asked a second time, but
again his father said nothing. So he asked a third time, and
in an outburst of fury, his father turned against Nachiketas
and cried, "I will give you to Death himself!"

Nachiketas instantly found himself at the great gates that
guard the castle of Yama, god of Death. There he waited. No
one came until three days later, when suddenly Death appeared in person. He was very embarrassed.

"You are a sacred guest to my house and a Brahmin besides, but I have kept you waiting here for three nights without hospitality," Yama said. "To make amends, therefore, I
will grant you three wishes. Name them."

At this point, Indian children have no idea what Nachiketas will ask for, but we were very glad to hear his first wish.

"May my father no longer be angry with me," he said. "May
he remember me and welcome my return home. That is my
first wish."

"It is done," replied Yama. "Your father will remember you
and rejoice that you have escaped the clutches of Death. Now
he will once again sleep in peace."

Nachiketas then revealed that he was not an ordinary boy.

"I know that there is no fear in Heaven," he said. "Old age

and Death are not there. The good who have gone there are rejoicing, being beyond both of these and also untouched by hunger, thirst, or sorrow. They are immortal. You, O Death, know the sacred fire that leads to Heaven. Explain the path to me. That is my second wish."

At this, Death was overjoyed, since he never expected such an apt pupil ever to appear at his door. He delivered a long catechism to Nachiketas which children block out or which Indian grandmothers mercifully abbreviate. Mine did. The gist of it, when you consult the written version, is contained in a lovely expression: "The fire that leads to Heaven is hidden in the secret place of the heart."

There is also this passage: "And Death told him about the fire of Creation, the beginning of all worlds." But the rest — a great deal of praise for orthodox sacrifices on the altar of the sacred fire — almost no one in India comprehends. The rituals themselves are too old for our memory, and Death's secret understanding is lost on us now. Nachiketas, however, understood the answer Yama gave, and he repeated the teachings to engrave them on his heart.

"A great doubt exists about what happens when a man dies," the boy continued. "Some say that he is, some say that he is not. Teach me the truth. That is my third wish."

Death could not believe his ears! He had been asked the one secret he would not divulge. "There was a time when even the gods did not know how to resolve this doubt. The law of life and death is mysterious. Release me from this boon," he cried.

But clever Nachiketas would not. He knew that the secret of life and death was the greatest knowledge to be gained, and he had come to its greatest teacher. Death at first refused to relent.

"Take horses and gold, cattle and elephants," he implored. "Take sons and grandsons who shall live a hundred years. I will give you vast lands and a life that lasts as long as you command. Take any wish you consider equal to what you have asked. Rule the earth. I will give you everything."

Nachiketas turned down all of these, but to keep up the suspense, Yama offered him innumerable fair maidens, chariots of war, and musical instruments to delight his days. However hard to obtain, any desire in earthly life could be his. Of course, as children we never believed that Nachiketas would fall for any of it. And he didn't.

"All of these pleasures pass away," he declared. "They only weaken the power of life. Man cannot be satisfied with material wealth. How can he enjoy life at all, knowing that Death is at the end of it? Can we be happy while you are so close to us? When a man is sure of his own immortality, then he will be ready to ask for a life of pleasure. I have no other wish. I can only ask for the wish I have named."

When Nachiketas raised himself up to this great speech, we were all thrilled. Triumph! Grandmother took great delight in painting Death as proud Death, and we always pressed her along the way for more details of how terrible and lordly he looked. Now Death was not proud any longer. Nachiketas had made him humble.

What Death said in reply to this wish, however, is not easy to comprehend. As a child, I only gathered that he was reassuring: little boys should not worry about the unhappy parts of life. One day we would grow up to discover a deeper truth, that the soul is immortal and cannot be claimed by Death.

That was the way it was told to me. The actual Upanishadic text gives the means of discovering this truth: not through sacrifice or devotion, not through any action or reasoning, but through knowing the Self, or *atman*, directly, man can gain power over everything in creation, including Death itself. Since no practical method is given, however, this may seem like rather a poor answer to wrest from Lord Death after you have pinned and vanquished him. But I was not disappointed. Apparently Death held the same orthodox opinions as my grandmother.

The world my grandmother described in her stories was not simply real to her, it was the supreme reality. Nachiketas was not a little boy, but the eternal knower residing in the heart of every person. My grandmother did not know how to realize the Self, but she clung to vestiges of faith in it, as was common in her generation. Except for a few unspoiled people, I doubt that anyone much shares her beliefs today.

The contrast between her and Uncle was the contrast between love and doubt, between the melting heart and the unconcerned intellect. They are like alien worlds to one another. After my exposure to Uncle, I didn't become a Communist or even an atheist. Nevertheless, I chose his world absolutely and as a matter of course. I don't know why anyone is motivated to choose skepticism, doubt, and mistrust over the more innocent values. They just seem irresistible.

The famous Scottish psychiatrist R. D. Laing has written about the day he learned there was no Santa Claus. As I recall, he was eight or nine, sitting at the breakfast table sipping his tea and saying how lovely Christmas was because of Santa Claus. His parents looked at him and said casually, "But Ronny, you're old enough to know that there is no Santa Claus, not really." He was shocked, and from that moment on he realized he hated them. He couldn't help it, any more than he could help it that he grew. It didn't matter that he had loved them before. Now he felt hatred for their sham truths and petty evasions. For him it was a sad, ridiculous, and unforgettable moment. He was launched on his way to becoming an adult.

Once the new angle is taken, it is very hard to turn back. The things I saw around me absolutely confirmed my unbelief, as well as my dedication to science as the best way to live in this world. The scriptures may promise that perfection can be realized and death turned into our servant, but the sickness and suffering we all experience tell something quite different. There is too great a gap between the fearless world delivered to Nachiketas and the troubled one we live in.

Mrs. MacNamara did not stay with us forever. Anne, the older sister of Terence and Philip, became quite sick and kept vomiting all the time. They took her to the army hospital, where my father examined her. He took a sample of urine, and it turned out that she was pregnant. It also turned out that Uncle was the father.

Until then, my father had resisted the suggestions from my mother and grandmother that our Anglo-Indians find another place to live. Now he had no other choice. We never saw them again, though I heard vaguely, many years later, that Terence and Philip took jobs with the railway. I hated Uncle for a while, but after he disappeared over the horizon I often wished him back with us. Scoundrel though he was, he was my first real teacher. He showed me, and no mistake, the castle of Death. He set me on the path.

4

The Ten-Rupee Brain

ONE DAY in physiology class we buried a saint. He was not one of the corpses the sweepers brought in to sell to the anatomy department of our medical school. I had bought one of those myself, a skeleton actually, for thirty-six rupees, or about four dollars. Since my particular interest lay in internal medicine, I tossed in ten rupees extra — less than a dollar by current rates of exchange — and received a brain, too, which I took back to my room for study.

The saint, however, was alive. We did not particularly revere him. In the Indian fashion he was called "saint" as an ordinary term — the word is applied to holy men more casually than in the West. He had walked down from the Himalayas at the invitation of Professor Nanda, who taught physiology to the younger medical students, the first- and second-year classes. Every course lasted three semesters, and if the lectures followed the traditional pattern (presumably laid down in London, circa 1900), the hours in class were excruciatingly long.

But Professor Nanda was a lively, inquisitive man who could teach a student how to detect the eight phases of a single heartbeat. He had also attended a lecture on meditation when I was a first-year student. It was 1964, and all at once such lectures were in the air. The curiosity about meditation in the West had reached India, curving back on itself, as it were. Whenever I got invited to the most "sophisticated" evening parties, someone would play a Beatles record, and we eagerly caught the allusions to bliss and Brahman. They had apparently become part of a tantalizing ethos in the West which included acid trips and radical protest, about which we knew nothing. We were completely surprised that India had contributed an ingredient to the mix. A part of our lives we took as much for granted as the devotional processions on the way to school suddenly jumped into a glamorous spotlight.

The lecture on meditation that Professor Nanda attended led him to become intrigued, not as a devotee but as a scientist. He had heard of the remarkable control over the body which advanced practitioners were said to have achieved. In India, all the wandering *sadhus, sanyasis,* swamis, and fakirs are accepted as part of the passing scene, to be believed in or not. As a rule, the choice is automatic: the devout believe while others do not. Professor Nanda decided to inject the note of experimentation, to discover what in reality a saint could accomplish.

The saint we buried was dressed in the faded saffron robes of a wandering monk, an ascetic. His matted hair and beard were untrimmed. His body bore the sacred marks of *bashma,* or holy ash. He had been exposed to the weather for many years. I don't remember anything at all about his spiritual presence. Naturally, I knew that he lived for spiritual attainment. I placed that in a peculiar category rather like astrology, a primitive profession that belonged to another India, even though relics of it survived. Given enough time, science would sweep away the saints, but it reserved some curiosity about their heart rate, breathing capacity, and blood levels of CO_2.

As a curiosity, this saint was very obliging. Professor Nanda placed him in a wooden box just large enough for him to sit inside in lotus posture. As the top was nailed on, we caught a last glimpse of him, half lidded and immobile as he began to meditate. Then the box was lowered into a pit dug especially for the purpose in one courtyard of the school. Dirt was thrown over the top while the physiology students looked on. After the box was well out of sight, there seemed nothing else to do. We gradually made our way back to the dorms to resume what we usually did, which was memorize.

Burying a holy man may seem a peculiarly Indian thing to do, but the most Indian thing about my medical training was memorization—we spent hundreds of hours at it. In my first three semesters I memorized the human anatomy in endless and useless detail, as every student before me had done who survived the rigors of the system. Two or three of us would gather in my room at night, peering at the tiny grooves in every bone of the skeleton I had purchased. Each groove had a name, and we would not be passed on to the next phase of school until we knew them all by heart.

Much of our time was spent this way over the course of the next four and a half years, which was divided into three "professional phases" lasting three terms each. At the end of each phase came a long battery of tests called practical examinations. They were terrifying because they came only once, and if you failed, you were sent back to the same classes in which you had just spent three semesters.

Some students had actually become legends of failure. They were primarily foreigners taken by the All-India Medical Institute as part of its mandate to educate doctors from all parts of the Third World. Lavish donations from American foundations came to the school on these terms. We enjoyed the best visiting lecturers, also American, who flew to Delhi directly from UCLA or Mount Sinai Hospital in New York. These professors had not been indoctrinated in the grind of rote memorization, so they came as a relief to us. One American succeeded in sparking my interest in biochemistry, one of the deadliest bores in the curriculum, when he walked into class the first day and announced, "If you were God, how would you design the molecules of a fat cell?"

Every class had fifteen assorted non-Indians from Malaysia, Kenya, Uganda, and elsewhere. One wealthy Fijian, who was famous for giving parties year in and year out, had failed the anatomy exam nine times. He was thirty-two years old and still a first-year student until a new professor passed him out of sheer disgust.

We Indian students were determined to work hard and pass our practical exams the first time. I can remember nights when I studied so long that I woke up with bones in my bed. My ten-rupee brain was also being dissected little by little, lasting well into my third year. By that time we had reached the region known as the reptilian brain, the tattered destination of a long journey that had already covered the cerebrum, cerebellum, medulla, hypothalamus, and hippocampus. Once my family rushed me off to the Himalayas to save me from the permanent daze of unending rote work, but I plunked my reptilian brain into a jar of formalin and took it along.

My first months at school still stick in my nostrils. Following the British system, we went directly from high school to medical school, skipping undergraduate college. This meant that at age seventeen I walked into the dissection hall, faced with fifteen or twenty cadavers. These were to be our companions for eighteen months and so stank of the formalin they were preserved in that I immediately lost my appetite for three months. When I got to the point of desperation, I took to chewing *paan* as a restorative for hunger.

Paan is a small green leaf wrapped around a pungent bit of betel nut, lime peel, and tobacco. It is taken after meals, generally by adults much older than I who are often half addicted. But being a medical student who reeked of corpses gave me special dispensation. My teeth acquired the characteristic brown stain of the *paan* chewer after about a week, and my appetite returned somewhat. As it happened, fifteen of the thirty-five Indian students in my class were girls. As a result of standing next to them over the dissection tables, I could not approach sitting with a girl for years without the certainty that she was wearing formalin instead of perfume.

By the time we came to the end of our third semester and took the first set of exams, we were prepared to write fifteen-page essays on the course of the radial or ulnar nerve as it ran down the arm, but we had not yet actually seen a living patient. After passing this obstacle, a student went to the second professional phase, which was devoted to pharmacology, microbiology, pathology, and an amorphous subject known as social and preventive medicine.

This was a code word for one topic: birth control. In the political climate of that time, the government strongly supported sterilization for men and contraceptive implants, or IUDs, for women in order to stem India's huge population growth. Mrs. Gandhi risked much of her political capital to popularize sterilization among the peasants, but the idea was hostilely received. As medical students, we were expected to align ourselves with the official policy; otherwise, the class had very little content, no more than a few scattered lectures on nutrition and hygiene for underdeveloped countries. Since most of us harbored a strong desire to escape to a developed country as soon as humanly possible, we did not pay serious attention to even the desultory presentations being delivered.

The second professional phase brought, if anything, a heavier burden of memorization than the first. This was thanks to pharmacology, which was taught quite strangely. In anatomy class we at least saw the bones whose names we memorized. The professor would twiddle with the small ones and toss them up in the air as he droned on. But pharmacology was like being lost entirely in a wilderness of words. We memorized the properties of hundreds of drugs, but we never actually saw any of them or administered them to patients. For each drug — say, digitalis — we learned the common and pharmaceutical names, the origin, specific action on the heart and other organs, correct dosage, toxicity in animals as well as humans, and a long list of side effects. In the case of digitalis, they began with nausea and ended with death.

Pathology turned out to be basically a repeat of physiology, except that instead of looking at healthy tissue through our miscroscopes, we looked at diseased ones. I actually found this enjoyable, since the professor did not simply dwell on necrotic tissue but talked about the processes of pathology that cause normal cells to become diseased. Following the course from normal, healthy functioning to the slight impairments that finally ended in a breakdown for the cell gave me a deep respect for the subtle causes of illness and the many stages that precede the appearance of symptoms. I found that I could be perfectly happy in a lab.

Our next block of finals, the second practical examinations, were quite elaborate. They included long essays, personal interviews, multiple-choice questions, and verbal examinations by the faculty, or viva voces.

These vivas were a particular strain on our nerves. Their ritual was absolutely unvarying. The candidate walked into a room where he met his two examiners. One was his own professor, who was called the internal examiner; the other was a professor in the same subject but from another medical school. This person, called the external examiner, routinely tried to fail as many candidates as possible in order to show the superiority of his own university; conversely, the internal examiner took a protective role with his own pupils. To crown the scene, a row of ten young postgraduate doctors were lined up behind the examiners' desk. They attended largely in the spirit of having fun at our expense.

When I entered the exam room for pharmacology, I saw

the external examiner poised with a *gulab jamun* halfway to his mouth. A *gulab jamun* is a sweetcake soaked in syrup, provided in an attempt to mollify the visiting professor. This man was more than the usual terror. His table was therefore lined with plates of sweets, *paan*, and little meat-stuffed *samosas*. As soon as his eye caught me and the poised sweetcake was just going down, he asked, "What is the most serious side effect of INH?"

I froze and my professor turned pale. The external examiner had unexpectedly asked me one of the easiest questions imaginable. INH, or Isoniazid, is one of the most common drugs used in India to treat tuberculosis, which is one of the most common diseases there. Even though I had never seen a case of TB, or a dose of INH for that matter, I certainly knew the answer.

But I had drawn a blank. I entered these exams with my heart pounding two hundred beats a minute and cotton in my mouth — a few missed questions on a viva meant months of wasted labor. I also couldn't help but notice that one of the postgraduate doctors was having what appeared to be a seizure. One side of his face began to twitch and went slack. At about the same time another postgraduate stuck his arm into the aisle as stiff as a plank, and a third kicked one leg into the air. I knew that they were trying to give me hints, but the message was lost on me.

The external examiner cocked an ironic glance at the internal examiner, and I recall that he actually said, "Did this student learn the most common side effect of the most common drug for treating the most common disease in the course?" Or at least we all read his thoughts. Then I blurted out, "Peripheral neuritis, sir." My professor relaxed, and the row of postgraduates returned to health. They had all been mimicking one sort of paralysis or another, which is indeed the worst effect of the drug—a progressive loss of sensation in the limbs that eventually leaves them paralyzed.

At the end of three years, with two practical exams passed,

the third professional phase began. For the first time we made rounds of patients in the wards and were assigned eight of them to work up under the supervision of an intern. I turned twenty-one and found that I had a special liking for internal medicine. This formed a third of our studies for the last year and a half. The rest was occupied with surgery and obstetrics, but in my case they definitely did not take hold.

Actually, my experience in obstetrics was quite benign. Whenever I was on duty, I was expected to sleep in the maternity ward, waiting for deliveries. At the crucial moment a *dai*, or midwife, would wake me up, and I would go to the lying-in room. Since the *dai* had already been there doing all the work that really needed doing, the only thing left for me was to stand sleepily in front of the mother and catch the baby when it came out. Our *dais* were wonderful, patient souls who loved caring for us as much as their charges. It was soothing to work with them. I would sometimes come to in mid-delivery, half asleep on my feet at three in the morning, to feel the *dai* nudging me from behind and clucking gently, as much for my benefit as the mother's.

To pass this course, each of us was required to deliver thirty-five normal and ten abnormal births. The difference between the two was determined solely by the baby's position in the womb, which is called its presentation. The *dai* was trained to tell this by pressing on the mother's belly. If she could feel that the baby was going to be born head first, then it was a normal delivery. Any fetus that was in a face, shoulder, or breech presentation was considered abnormal.

In these situations, the *dais* performed an intricate and delicate series of manipulations that allowed them to turn the baby into the normal position. Therefore, we had to worry about a minimum of actual abnormal deliveries. The manipulations were supposed to be the doctor's terrain, too, but the *dai* was the expert. She would cover my hands with hers to guide me through the necessary motions. Any wrong moves

ran a serious risk — a baby could be injured in the womb or
even strangled with the umbilical cord. However, this almost
never happened, thanks to the *dai*. It was absurdly easy for
the student doctor to get his forty-five certificates of delivery
signed, and unlike American obstetrics today, almost no Cae-
sarean sections were required.

With so little to do in the maternity ward, I shied away out
of boredom. My term in surgery, on the other hand, was a
fiasco. On the first day, we were assigned to scrub and assist
one of the surgery faculty, a tall, bearded Sikh. It was quite
strange to see him standing over his patient wearing the large
turban that Sikhs never remove; in this instance it was criss-
crossed with green surgical cloth. The surgeon, who was
named Dr. Singh, motioned me to his side to assist. For first-
term surgery students, "assist" means that you hold a retrac-
tor in place without moving for three hours. Three of us had
been assigned to this particular procedure, which was a kidney operation. The other two students were standing opposite me with their retractors. I moved in to take mine, and in
doing so I lightly touched the sleeve of Dr. Singh's surgical
gown with one finger of my glove.

Without saying a word, he straightened up and left the
room. Through the window in the door we saw him slowly
remove his gown, repeat a complete scrub of arms and hands,
and put on a new pair of gloves. He returned to the patient,
but for some reason I had not caught on to the point of his
demonstration in sterile technique. Since I had never seen a
live kidney exposed for surgery, I leaned in eagerly. The finger of my glove once again touched the surgeon's sleeve. Dr.
Singh was famous at school for his composure, but he turned
to me with a black look.

"You there," he said, "don't touch me again, and from now
on stand aside."

He then left the O.R. and repeated the entire procedure
again. I was fairly disoriented before that moment, but then

I lost my nerve completely. As I was standing behind him, unable to see a thing that was going on around the kidney, my glance fell on a black rubber disc on the floor and I idly stepped on it. Suddenly sparks flew, and Dr. Singh jumped — his hand had received a mild electrical shock. I had shorted out the special knife he used to cauterize blood vessels during surgery.

He called a halt to the operation and took me aside. "You are not a surgery student," he said. "You are just a bull in my china shop. You needn't bother to return."

I never did. In order to pass the exam, I read surgical textbooks for hours in my room, falling back on my ability to memorize, which by this time was practically fantastic. On the day the vivas came around, three semesters later, I could rattle off the configuration and use of instruments I had never held and describe in minute detail surgical procedures I had never seen, much less followed.

In my last year I was happily entrenched in the hospital routine, spending every day on the wards. Many of our patients were rural villagers. They came to Delhi for care usually only as a last resort after the traditional means had failed to cure them. We had absolutely no respect for the folk medicine that the village doctors practiced or that the patient tried on himself. At an Indian medical school, the one thing you are guaranteed not to learn about is Indian medicine. But I was drawn to these patients, who looked at me as if I came from a higher world. In reality I had been assigned the drudgery of physical exams, which the staff doctors were more than happy to shirk. But since my schedule in internal medicine was very light, I soon fell into the habit of visiting my patients when I had free time.

They liked me to come by just before the evening curry was dished out. The twilight hour is the loneliest in every hospital I have ever worked in. There was usually no conversation. We realized implicitly that I knew nothing of the life of a sandalmaker or woodcutter, just as they knew nothing of a doctor's. Sitting with them was enough. If I happened to come by after dinner, a patient and I might sit in the ward without saying a word until darkness fell and we could see the glimmering home fires sprinkled across the city.

This small attention comforted them a great deal. Since our hospital was the most advanced teaching facility in the country, it was staffed by many academic doctors. They always made rounds trailed by a gaggle of white-coated medical students. When the entourage showed up at the bedside of a sick villager, someone who had never set foot in a hospital before and was appalled to find himself in one now, the academic doctor hardly asked his name. He would launch into a discourse about the etiology and progress of the disease in question, while the students hoped either to make the brilliant remark that decided the case or else to be mercifully passed over in silence. After thirty minutes of this, the group trotted off to their next case, leaving the villager utterly bewildered.

I wonder how much harm we were doing them by this pretense that they were invisible. Our patients were incredibly trusting and sometimes beautifully simple people. Taking them to a city hospital was as cruel as ripping fledglings from the nest. In America it is rare to see any display of vulnerability. Everyone has grown used to being a stranger among strangers, and if he has the misfortune to go into the hospital, he knows automatically how to put up a front. But Indian villagers have no experience with isolation. They open their eyes at birth to see their mother, grandmother, sisters, and aunts. In all probability, this will be the smallest circle of family they ever experience until they die.

One day, however, a woman of a very different type was admitted. She was around fifty, quite dignified in manner, and in her face was a special quality Indians call *sattva*. *Sattva* is translated as virtue or purity, but what is unmistakable in sattvic people is their inner light. This woman radiated *sattva* in a very innocent and unself-conscious way, even though she had apparently suffered quite a severe stroke.

Her family soon came to visit her, and I discovered that one of her nieces was a girl I knew. Her name was Rita, and our parents had a quaint connection. When my father was in England after the war, he went to a military club in London and by chance met an officer in the air force whose last name was also Chopra. They struck up a conversation and after a few minutes discovered that they had both been married on the same day. This coincidence made a big impression on both men, partly because of astrology, which all Indians consult before setting their wedding day, but mostly because both were newlyweds who had taken reluctant leave of their wives just a few months before.

The two Chopras remained friends after that, but I had set eyes on Rita only a few times, once when I was thirteen and her mother gave me a ride home from school. She took pity on me when she saw me standing out in the rain, waiting to take the bus home after a cricket match. Several of us boys were allowed to climb into her car, and I found myself, muddy and hot, sitting next to a lovely girl who was impeccably out-fitted in her convent school uniform.

Rita's face, shyly turned toward the car window, became mixed up in my mind with that moment — it must have been my first encounter with adult self-consciousness — but when I later saw her sitting in the front row of a college debate tournament, I was terribly pleased. Debating had become a love of mine in medical school, and I took enormous pride in winning matches, although we usually debated ridiculous things. For example, one topic read, "The house is resolved that Christopher Columbus went too far." In India, the relations between young people of the opposite sex are incredibly chaste by Western standards, and just these two glimpses of Rita seemed to me like romance.

Her aunt, as it turned out, had not had a stroke but rather a serious and progressive disease attacking the nervous system, and she was kept in the hospital for more than a year. Since Rita and her family frequently came to visit, I began to see her more often and eventually to talk to her. We were both shy, and behind our backs the two mothers fretted that nothing would come of this contact but friendship. In friendship they had no interest, but they decided to wait.

In my graduation year school was going very well. By dint of continual grinding, I passed my examinations in the top five for every subject except surgery. Now that we were actually involved with patients, I was thriving, and I fully expected to graduate with distinction. My professors looked on me with great pride, too, but we were all to be terribly disappointed. My fall, which was nearly complete, came at the hands of an external examiner at the last viva of medical school.

When the time for the practical examination came, letters were sent out all over northern India to patients who were known to have unusual conditions, and they were paid a few rupees to come to the institute. Each candidate was assigned to one of these patients. He first sat alone with the patient and made a thorough examination. Then the two examiners would enter the room. They would ask the student for his findings in the case, then he could proceed to his diagnosis and proposed method of treatment.

I was assigned a patient who exhibited a series of peculiar and apparently unconnected findings. During the physical I noticed that his palate had an unusually high, arched shape, and the feet also had high arches. His reflexes were hyperactive, and I noticed an abnormal heart rhythm. This, along with other signs, told me that his heart was slightly enlarged, leading to congestive heart failure; he also exhibited what are known as focal neurological findings.

Summing all of these up, I felt a sudden thrill. I was certain that my patient was suffering from Friedrich's ataxia, a disorder so rare that our longest textbooks devoted perhaps four lines to it. It was nearly five in the afternoon by then, and when the two examiners came in, it was obvious that they were very tired. The external examiner turned to me and, skipping all the preliminaries, said, "What's your diagnosis?"

My own professor looked alarmed. "Don't you want to hear the findings first?" he asked. But this only made the visitor stubborn.

"What is your diagnosis?" he repeated. I had no choice.

"Friedrich's ataxia, sir," I said.

He burst out with a harsh laugh. "Come on now, who told you?" he asked me. He thought that one of the postgraduate doctors, who were notorious for helping out the candidates, had tipped me off. I was completely unable to convince him that I had made the diagnosis on my own, and after a few minutes he said angrily, "I will tolerate almost anything from a student except lying," and with that he announced that I had failed.

My professor argued with the external examiner for half an hour while I sat by miserably. The man would not budge. It was finally settled that I could take the exam again, but the failing mark stood against me. My second patient was a case of rheumatic fever, which I diagnosed correctly, but the damage had been done, and I was awarded a simple "pass" without distinction.

I have done my best to set down these experiences accurately and to describe the sort of education I received in becoming a physician. It was a psychologically precarious time, and it was not relieved at graduation when our commencement speaker told us, "Now you have a license to heal, but it is also a license to kill." At the same time, a foolish provincial arrogance had been instilled in us. We considered it our professional badge. The All-India Medical Institute took such pains not to be an Indian medical school that it turned out to be very Indian in the end. The topmost layer of modern science, with the jet-set American faculty, was laid over the hulk of an antiquated British system, largely unchanged since Victoria's death. And that in turn tottered on a chaotic pile of Indian customs that no one could escape.

I came out of it all desperate to prove my skill, which to me meant going to America. Because of the brain drain from India to the West, the government had banned the standardized test that a doctor had to take to qualify for practicing medicine overseas. Students from my school were forced to fly to Sri Lanka and sit for the exam there. In 1970 I went and took the test, just after the village posting I describe in the next chapter. Since I didn't want to waste my whole trip on one examination, I visited some sights, including a famous temple built around Buddha's tooth.

As I left the temple, I decided, simply on impulse, to buy a necklace from one of the vendors in the arcade. I took it back to Delhi, and the next time I saw Rita, I took it out of my pocket and asked her to marry me. She said yes and burst into tears. Our mothers were so relieved that they frantically called each other to announce the joyful news, but in their excitement, and with the state of the telephones, they got only busy signals for the next eight hours. Very soon afterward Rita and I exchanged rings. We went directly from the wedding to the hospital to visit her aunt, to thank her for the part she had played in our future together. Within a few months, this gracious woman was dead.

I have not forgotten the saint we buried in physiology class. After six days, Professor Nanda met us in the courtyard again, and workmen began to unearth the saint's box. This took almost half an hour while we waited in curious anticipation. The box was lifted out, then the top pried off, and after some minutes the saint slowly stood up. His eyes were still half-lidded. He gave us a little wave but no smile. I wish now I could remember the expression on his face at that remarkable moment.

The saint was escorted into the physiology lab, where he

politely asked for a glass of warm milk. He sipped it calmly as he was hooked up to the various monitors. Professor Nanda had already determined that the pulse and breathing were unusually faint when the saint was immersed in meditation. His heartbeat at first sounded nonexistent, but on closer hearing it was in fact fluttering in light, very rapid throbs, like a bird's heart. The saint could enter this state at will, as he showed us in the lab. The EKG, or electrocardiogram, confirmed his heartbeat by faint squiggles traced out on graph paper. Other tests showed a level of reduced oxygen consumption that no bodily mechanism we had studied could account for. The simple fact was that the saint had lived peacefully for six days under conditions that would have destroyed a normal mind and body in less than twelve hours.

All of us were amazed by this demonstration, but after a week it was forgotten. The saint slowly walked away from our school. Within an hour I'm sure he once again felt the warm sand of pilgrimage beneath his feet. We thus missed a perfect opportunity to ask ourselves what "normal" really means in the functioning of the human physiology.

Studies have repeatedly validated such feats as we witnessed, but the few I have read were dryly clinical in their approach. I suspect that they mirror the same shallow curiosity we showed.

I did not yet realize what deep footprints our saint was leaving behind. It would take ten years before I had a significant encounter with meditation. For the moment, I was still engrossed with my ten-rupee brain. I would give a great deal now to know more about the content of that saint's mind and its wisdom. About his soul, the most important thing to him, a deeper silence prevails. In our arrogance, we thought that a saint could be captured on graph paper. But his quiet heart kept its secrets.

5

Landing on the Moon

"Bleeding! bleeding! bleeding!" Ghanshyam practically shrieked at me. He waved wildly in the direction of the
village. I must come with him.

I have worked with calmer orderlies than Ghanshyam. He
was good for throwing buckets of water on the walls of our
dispensary. We did that to keep down the unbearable heat.
He could hold one end of a bandage while I wrapped a farm-
er's foot after a bullock stepped on it. But he was absolutely
hopeless in emergencies. I suspected at times that he must
be the village halfwit.

"What's the matter, anyway?" I asked with irritation. I stood
up in the stream and walked to shore. All my clothing — one
pair of khaki shorts, actually — lay under a shady grove of
trees. I put them on.

Ghanshyam was so disturbed he couldn't answer. He ran
a few paces toward the village and then back to me, his turban unwinding as he ran. He was so out of breath he could
only say "Bleeding, bleeding!" in broken gasps. It was naturally a bit unnerving. We both trotted off toward the end of
the village where he had been pointing. After a bit I got some
more information out of him.

"Dr. Sahib Khan is in trouble!" he cried. Saleem Khan was my partner at the dispensary. As soon as I realized that he was the one who wanted me, I knew that a serious complication must have arisen with one of our cases. We were both fledgling doctors, about twenty-three years old, and assigned here together by our medical school. It was our responsibility to take care of an entire village. An instructor from the medical school stopped by every three or four days with supplies. Otherwise, we were on our own.

When I turned toward the dispensary, Ghanshyam pulled my arm and pointed to Sarla's house instead. Just what I had imagined: Sarla was a seventeen-year-old girl whom we had examined that morning. She was pregnant, very near term, and had been forced to come to us by her husband, a bricklayer who worked in nearby Ghaziabad. That day he had missed his ride on the lorry and brought his wife in to us, complaining that she seemed sick all the time and had no energy.

Sarla certainly looked sick. Suspecting anemia, we gave her some iron pills. Her husband had walked in asking for a "blood tonic" for his wife. He reluctantly agreed to allow her to take the pills instead. We told her that after her baby came, she should make the trip to Delhi, about eighty miles away, for a kind of blood test called a hemogram. He refused to let her consider the blood test. We weren't too surprised. Most of the villagers were quite hesitant to take our medicines at all.

Poor Saleem, I thought. It must be a breech delivery. The local midwives, the *dais*, wouldn't be calling in a Western-style doctor unless complications had arisen. I hoped he remembered his manipulation procedures. Ghanshyam rushed into the house ahead of me. I stopped on the threshold for a second, surveying the room. On a wide, comfortable-looking bed lay two people. One was Sarla, sitting up with a soft, loving smile on her face and a newborn infant sucking at her breast. The other was Saleem, lying half-fainted in a pool of blood.

"What's wrong. What's happening here?" I asked in English.

"Probably vasovagal syncope," Saleem said, sitting up. He was still pale, almost ghostly looking, but he was recovering.

"Oh," I said. I never knew that he couldn't stand the sight of blood.

"Dr. Sahib has fainted," put in the midwife. I had overlooked her entirely until she spoke. She looked both kind and proud. At one and the same time she had delivered a difficult baby — it had been a breech birth, after all — and resuscitated the doctor, too. "He cut his lip when he fell."

I could see that she was finishing with a bandage for Saleem's mouth. She offered him a glass of warm milk to make him feel steadier. He declined, with an open look of admiration in his eyes, and turned to get me out of there. I couldn't blame him. We congratulated the new mother and the midwife. Saleem usually found it hard to tolerate the ignorance of our villagers, but for a few days he didn't touch on that.

Our village, named Ramgarh, was little more than a cluster of mud huts surrounded by wheat fields. I had no idea how old Ramgarh was. It looked immortal, as though untouched by the centuries, but its population was dwindling rapidly. The younger men were fed up with walking behind their bullocks in the fields. Very few of the farmers actually owned a field, except for the handful of village landlords, all of whom were old. The future beckoned from the larger towns like Ghaziabad, so naturally that was where the young men went.

Our dispensary was built of brick, but, like all the other buildings, its floor was made of cow and buffalo dung. Dung serves very well as a flooring. It is clean enough to use in kitchens. It can be replaced every season with a new surface at no cost, and it greets the nose with a sharp, refreshing smell after it has cured in the hot, dry air. Saleem and I had been assigned to a rotation in Ramgarh for six months as part of our internship. We had a large enough house, complete with a courtyard and a servant to cook our meals.

The work was blissfully easy. For one thing, we had almost no medicines to work with and no equipment at all. We arrived with our black bags, a copy of Harrison's *Principles of Internal Medicine*, and the usual few pharmaceuticals you take to the countryside — iron pills, anti-tubercular pills, and anti-helminth pills. (Helminths are parasitic worms very common to the tropics but almost unknown in the West.) Our villagers showed a very high incidence of tuberculosis. If anyone came to the dispensary looking half dead and wasted, we automatically gave out the antitubercular pill and usually the iron pill as well.

Most of the villagers did not believe in our prescriptions. They had relied for centuries on other ways, primarily the knowledge of the local Ayurvedic vaidya. His advice was the ultimate authority, along with the village elder's, and his herbs were the ultimate cure. Saleem, who was already showing his brilliance in microbiology, was not suited for village life. He hated the absence of air conditioning (so did I) and the feeble, twinkling electricity. He hated the ignorance of these farmers who preferred to call in a grandmother and a midwife when a baby was due, rather than a doctor, and who stubbornly rejected our explanations about germs because they all knew that men got sick because demons got into them.

But a village posting is a perfect place to decelerate from the grind of med school. Saleem and I liked nothing better than to lie in the courtyard whenever the sun was bearable, generally in the late afternoon. We didn't move much or talk at all. The radio would be tuned to the cricket matches between Australia and India. We stared for long stretches at the swaying branches of the peepul trees, whose enormous heart-shaped leaves are good vehicles for self-hypnosis, and we forgot that we were doctors. It was just what we wanted.

Our last days in school were behind us. By any standard we were modern physicians; therefore, by Indian standards, we were absolutely elite physicians. To be a graduate of the All-India Medical Institute carried enormous prestige. None of that seemed very significant, however, once you left Delhi behind. Now that we were in Ramgarh, it meant nothing. If anything, what we noticed was how much our professors had failed to tell us.

The visiting lecturers from the West had everything to say about the latest modality for treating arthritis or chronic depression, as taught at Yale or Johns Hopkins. Cholera, however, is not commonly seen at either Yale or Johns Hopkins, so lectures on that subject were scarce, though cholera is never absent for long from India and fitfully rages into fearsome epidemics.

We also heard practically nothing about leprosy or elephantiasis, which are both endemic throughout the subcontinent. Some of the diseases we studied had all but disappeared. We were told that smallpox immunization had accomplished something unheard of in the course of our planet's evolution. It had wiped a strain of bacteria out of existence.

Last week that fact came to mind again as I watched a TV program about a medical team's desperate attempt to stop a rash of disease that had flared up in Bangladesh and threatened to sweep down the rivers with the native boatmen. The year of the outbreak must have been about 1983. Huge rewards were offered for anyone who could turn in a verified case of the disease. Squads of investigators combed the countryside. Every local train was being stopped to alert the passengers about the possible epidemic. Single unreported cases, escaping detection after everyone around them had been checked, caused hundreds of deaths in a few weeks. The medical team feared the worst but did not have the heart to dwell on it. What if the disease spread, as it could easily do, from Bangladesh to India, than quickly to Afghanistan, Iran, and eventually the entire continent of Africa? They were very anxious, and they had a right to be. The disease was smallpox.

· · ·

It was the summer of 1969 when we were posted to Ramgarh, and a striking thing happened soon after we arrived. Saleem had taken a short break to go to Delhi — to escape the boredom of the country life and to remind himself that air conditioning still existed. I couldn't blame him. The temperature hit 120 degrees almost every day. We would have Ghanshyam throw buckets of water, not just on the walls, but right onto the beds in our rooms before we crawled in to sleep. Few patients came to see us, so I spent my time down in the stream or padding around in bare feet and safari shorts.

One afternoon, when it was almost too stifling to move, Ghanshyam came to my room, almost hysterical. (This was before I got used to him.) "Dr. Sahib must come quick," he exclaimed. "The village elder has a grandson who has just gone mad." I pressed him for details, but there was only one idea in his head at a time. "He's gone mad," he muttered, "he's gone mad." We both ran toward the village elder's compound while I tried to recall as best I could the section on heat stroke in Harrison's *Principles*. The only thing I could think of was that the boy had become delirious from the heat.

"Do we have any ice?" I asked Ghanshyam. He shook his head.

"Only at the ice cream factory in Ghaziabad," he said. I couldn't bring myself to ask him to get on his bicycle and travel thirteen miles in the sun. I decided to examine the boy first. Inside the house when we arrived stood a group of people. The village elder approached, a dignified old man in his seventies with a pointed beard. He talked to me in a calm, assured voice.

"The boy's all right now. It was too much heat. He's still out of his head, but I'm sure he'll be all right when he is cooler. He thinks that there are men on the moon." He invited me to look at the boy.

I found him in the next room, lying naked on the bare floor while two women, probably his mother and aunt, lightly sponged him with cold water. He was about twelve. He looked comfortable, though my hand came away from his forehead a little hot. My first impulse was to sit him up to test him for cranial nerve function and motor or sensory deficits. But I felt awkward, and I didn't have any of the equipment with me, anyway.

"He has a little delirium," I told his grandfather when I came out. "He might say strange things for a while. It's common with heat stroke."

"He thinks there are men on the moon." The elder shook his head. "We always thought he was a little moonstruck."

That evening, when I turned on the radio for the cricket scores, I heard some news. The Americans had landed on the moon. Neil Armstrong had taken the first step. Pictures were coming back on TV. I couldn't make out much more than that. The reception from Delhi made it sound as if the announcer was on the moon with them. The next morning I rushed back to the village elder's house and told him that the boy was right. The elder was shocked.

"You have been to school," he protested, "and you believe such nonsense? You think there are men on the moon, too?"

I kept from laughing at him, and when he was slightly less incredulous, he convened a special meeting of the *panchayat*. These are the five men, mostly large landowners, who sit as the village council. One could see them, all over seventy, holding long discussions in the village elder's courtyard. They deliberated all important matters concerning Ramgarh. On the outskirts would be several old men, *ganja* addicts, smoking their hookahs, listening on, and falling into a semistupor. That was village life.

I described for the *panchayat* what I knew of the Soviet and American space programs. They listened to me, clearly baffled, not a little suspicious. Finally the elder spoke.

"We find what you say completely strange. How can it be that men of this earth have stepped onto the moon? But you

are educated, and stranger things have happened." He paused
for a moment. I could see them thinking about Hanuman,
the monkey king, who plucked up a mountain and flew back
with it to bring a single herb to Lord Rama. If he decided to
tell me the story, it would take a long time. He didn't.

"It may still be that you are mistaken," he said. "We only
hope that nothing bad comes out of this foolishness."

I laughed on the way home, and when I found Saleem in
his room, I told him the story. He was already grumpy from
having to abandon his air-conditioned study in Delhi. I got
to hear his opinion of such ignorance. A while later, I discovered that the elder's grandson had heard about the moon
landing when he walked to Ghaziabad that morning and
happened to take too much sun.

Another time, an older villager summoned us to his house to
see his son. We walked in and found him in the midst of a
seizure. He was about twenty-two, and while his father anx-
iously held him down, the son jerked and thrashed on his
bed. I could see him biting his tongue. He had lost control of
his bladder, and at intervals in the thrashing he seemed to
doze off. Saleem and I agreed that we were seeing an instance of epilepsy, what is called a grand mal seizure. Luckily
we had some phenobarbital in our bags, and we injected the
young man. His seizure subsided. Nothing happened all that
night, but the next day we heard that the patient, whose name
was Govind, started to have fits again.

I gave him another shot of phenobarbital while Saleem
rushed to Delhi to get the preferred drug for epilepsy, Dilantin. We administered both medications to Govind all that week.
The onset, duration, and character of his seizures followed
the textbook pattern. Most grand mal seizures are due to idiopathic epilepsy. (Idiopathic means "without cause.") Govind did not respond to treatment, however. This meant that
other conditions that can cause seizures had to be con-

sidered, such as a tumor in the brain. We were quite anxious for him. We had started him on twice the usual dosage of Dilantin; now we nearly doubled that and gave him considerably larger injections of phenobarbital as well. Govind kept having the seizures, and they started coming closer together. He was now having five or six of them a day. Moreover, he grew unsteady and found it hard to walk. This could have been due to a toxic reaction from the Dilantin, which is very powerful. But the possibility of a brain tumor became stronger.

We advised Govind's father to send his son to the medical school's hospital in Delhi. He would need a brain scan, EEGs, and then who knows what—surgery? radiation? But first he needed the tests. Govind's father refused. Instead, he called in an Ayurvedic doctor from Ghaziabad. We were disapproving but curious. What did the vaidya say?

"Vaidji says he has an imbalance of the *doshas*," the father informed us. *Doshas* are the three basic divisions of natural functioning which make up the material world, including the human body. After finding an imbalance in Govind, the Ayurvedic doctor recommended what he always did, a new diet and a few herbs. He told the family that all would be well in a few weeks. Saleem was bitter when he heard this and angry at the credulity of these people.

"Are you going to follow Vaidji's advice?" I asked the father.

"In time," he replied. "For now, it is in our hands." What did that mean? He didn't want to tell us what they were going to do. He did say that his great-uncle had suffered similar fits. Eventually the evil spirits inside him had had to be driven out. If we wanted to see what that entailed, we could come to the village square that night.

We witnessed a frightening ordeal. Govind was seated in a chair, bound hand and foot with ropes. Another rope secured him to the chair. As the villagers looked on, two men whipped him with lashes. Govind screamed in terror. The spectators watched in silence. I thought of rushing in to save Govind somehow, but the moment I began to edge through the crowd, an old man held me back.

"Be still," he said, "or the spirits will come back."

I went to see Govind the next morning. He was badly bruised from the night before, but he was smiling. The seizures had stopped. His father was jubilant.

"We have stopped all the medicines," he told me. Now they were ready to start with the vaidya's diet and herbs. Did Vaidji approve of the beating? The man smiled secretly. They didn't dare tell Vaidji, for fear that he would not give them the herbs.

The next time the vaidya visited Ramgarh, I saw that he was beaming over his patient's progress. He showed me some special herbs wrapped in a brown paper packet and began to pronounce Sanskrit terms that were meaningless to me. The herbs looked like sweepings from the floor of a tobacco shop. What about the beating? I asked him. Vaidji merely quoted from an Ayurvedic text, which said that anything in the world, absolutely anything, can serve as medicine if administered at the right time and in the right place.

"You don't think Govind had demons inside?" I asked.

Vaidji shrugged. "We could say there were impurities," he said.

"How would a beating drive them out?" I protested.

"How did they get in to begin with?" he replied.

After that, we did not have much interaction. The vaidya's comings and goings were an unobtrusive part of village life, as they had been forever. Although our patients regularly mixed visits to our dispensary with visits to the vaidya, we kept to our separate territories.

One time, however, on a weekend furlough to New Delhi, I sought out a bookstall that specialized in Ayurvedic texts. It was just a narrow slot, not much wider than my shoulders. I squeezed in past the shopkeeper, who sat stooped over an old book with his afternoon cup of spice tea.

The back room was dusty and badly lit, but I could see that I was surrounded from floor to ceiling by medical books. Most of them appeared to be in Sanskrit and had been written before the year A.D. 1000. After browsing for a few minutes, I got discouraged and left. The shopkeeper did not look up from his tea as I squeezed back out.

I waited four months for Govind's next seizure. It never came. A year later, back in Delhi and ready to go to America, I went back to Ramgarh. It had become a cherished spot to me. Saleem and I had often spent evenings walking to the neighboring village, where two of our classmates, also on a rural posting, would give us a good supper. One time, on the way over, the sky had filled with red light from one end to the other. That sunset became Ramgarh in my mind. Its wheat fields were like the floor of an immense crimson dome. As I got off the bus from Delhi, I saw the same fields and the dwindling mud huts. The sky was an immense blue dome that day. I looked for Govind, but he wasn't home. He had taken the bullocks to the fields to plow for the new seed. He had not had a seizure since I left.

I did not learn much about Ayurveda in Ramgarh. I learned a lot, however, about what medical care has to be. It has to suit the people a doctor cares for. It has to agree with their temperaments and what they expect from life. It must be affordable and humane. And it must work. It never occurred to me that Ayurveda would work. In its present form, although it blends in with the daily traditions and common beliefs of the people, the way of the vaidya seems greatly diluted from what it once must have been. In the ancient times, Ayurvedic doctors were paid only if they kept the people well, which they managed to do for thousands of years. But that era is far removed from the India of recent centuries.

The ancient texts of Ayurveda reveal an astonishing sophistication. Sushruta, the paramount authority on surgery, tells us explicitly about his techniques and even provides pictures of his tools. They look almost exactly like the scalpels and retractors of modern surgeons. Sushruta used to take the heart-shaped leaves of the peepul tree, the same kind I gazed at to hypnotize myself on a hot afternoon, and fashion them into models of noses. When one of these models satisfied him, he went to work. Sushruta possessed the skill to rebuild damaged or even lost noses. This delicate and painstaking procedure, called a rhinoplasty, does not reappear in medicine until modern plastic surgery. Sushruta's reputation still runs so high that American plastic surgeons have a society that goes by his name.

Sushruta also knew about the circulation of the blood. He could keep wounds from becoming septic. He submerged cadavers in clear, running streams and observed the fine details of anatomy as the water sloughed off layers of tissue. He seems in every respect to embody the deepest inquisitive spirit of a researcher and also a physician's most knowing skills. When exactly he lived is a matter for argument, but apparently it was many centuries before the birth of Christ.

There is something far more important about Sushruta than his position in the annals of the history of medicine. Few doctors, even among those who have heard of him, realize that his celebrated discourse on surgery comes at the end of his book, the *Sushruta Samhita*. He had far greater knowledge than just that. He understood every possible aspect of the art of healing, which means that he understood every aspect of man. He was, like Hippocrates, an angelic doctor. After many chapters on the spirit of healing, on medicines to extract from plants, on purifying diets and correct habits, Sushruta finally arrives at surgery only as the physician's last resort. After the doctor has failed, he must rely on surgery.

Sushruta bequeathed to Ayurveda a view that man is infinite in scope. He himself had a mind that displayed infinite qualities. More than a physician, he was a rishi, a seer. He had looked as deeply into Nature as our spirit can, and only then did he turn to ordinary work. Motivated by his own perfection, he approached patients, not as victims of malady, but as people who could potentially perfect themselves, too. That aspiration lies at the core of Ayurveda, and of course it is not seen, not on a large scale, in India today. She is too poor, too wretched, too afraid of the next epidemic that might sweep down the rivers. Sushruta and his perfection are as far away in time as the moon is in space.

But there is gravity to keep the moon from ever really escaping, and the same is true of Ayurveda. As tenuous as it may appear to us, the core of Ayurveda has not been lost. It may be that its most wonderful flowering has yet to occur. I have met the vaidyas and the modern rishis, who give me hope. More than hope. The potential is there for transforming the face of medicine entirely, and not just in India. All that is needed is to accept the possibility that such a change can take place, then to reach the depths where transformation is effortless and most powerful. Our servants wait on us, but they wait inside. Teilhard de Chardin gave us a wonderful glimpse of our future state: "The day will come when, after harnessing the winds, the tides, and gravitation, we shall harness for God the energies of love. And on that day, for the second time in the history of the world, man will have discovered fire."

And that day, for the second time, man will land on the moon.

6

Health and a Day

IT CAN BE VERY CONFUSING to tell health from sickness. In 1971 I was at the end of my internship in New Jersey and ready for a two-year residency in internal medicine. My sights were still fixed on Boston, in particular on a prestigious private hospital that is commonly referred to as the Mayo Clinic of the East. As an intern, my salary had been only $200 a month, but as a resident I could expect to make $500. I would be able to afford an apartment and the lowliest of cars. My wife, Rita, had also become pregnant three months after we settled in America. We were overjoyed.

I borrowed a friend's redoubtable VW bug and chugged up to Boston to interview with the prestigious clinic. It was established in a grand dowager of a brick building on one of the most high-toned stretches of Commonwealth Avenue. The shaded lane of oak trees outside was very unlike the parking lot in New Jersey. As soon as my shoes touched the carpet inside, I knew that no more local Mafiosi — checking for relatives with bullet wounds — would be frightening me when they came on their nightly check of the emergency room. A new stratum of American society was opening up to me. I didn't see the cover of *Time* magazine that often, but if I had, I would have recognized many of the patients who came here, most of them very quietly.

The interview went beautifully. The chief of medicine in my community hospital liked my work and wanted to do anything he could to keep me on. He said so in his recommendation, and the prestigious clinic must have been impressed. They wanted me. It was going to be a big jump.

However, in the midst of our jubilation over this stroke of fortune, Rita and I discovered that her health insurance would not cover the delivery of a baby if we moved from New Jersey. I made a worried call to Boston and was told that as a courtesy they would waive all doctor's fees if my wife cared to deliver in the prestigious clinic, but there was still the matter of $1,000 for the room charge. They could do nothing about that, even for a staff resident. We could take out Massachusetts insurance, but it would not cover any preexisting conditions. Being pregnant was definitely a pre-existing condition.

Where was the money to come from for our baby? I dreaded another two years of highway accidents and interested Mafiosi, but I had no credit to borrow against. I refused to tell my family in India that a doctor in America couldn't afford to deliver his own baby. Then it occurred to me that a flight to India was only $450 round-trip. I could swing that, just barely, by giving up my free night to work in the hospital emergency room. It paid $4 an hour, and I could stay there until I came on in the morning.

When I came up with this scheme, a close friend, also an intern, tried to talk me out of it. If my son was born in India, he said, he could never be president of the United States. Really? Yes, to be president you have to be born an American citizen and be at least thirty-five years old. Rita and I took this very seriously. My boy should have his chance to be president. But then we decided to go ahead with my plan.

We didn't tell my father anything until the week before I was due in Boston.

I called him at the last moment and explained that the new job demanded all my time. It wasn't fair to Rita. What she needed just then were quiet surroundings and a loving family. So I was sending her home on the next Air India flight. It sounded reasonable enough to me. My father's reaction was panic, naturally. But he agreed to it in the end, and I showed up in New York to put Rita on the flight. But Air India wouldn't take her. It was obvious, even to a ticket agent, that my wife was very, very pregnant. She could easily deliver on the plane, in fact. They weren't having any of it. We pleaded with the manager, who offered me a stack of release forms to fill out. I managed some skillful white lies in doctor language, and eventually I was permitted to see my Rita carried off in a jet. It was the moment when both of us wanted nothing more than to be together.

I started work the next day in Boston. The first weeks were terribly lonely for me. I had grown used to spending part of every day with Rita. When I was on night call, we would arrange to have lunch together in the hospital cafeteria. Rita waited for me there, even when I was an hour late. When I finally walked in, totally wrapped up in my last emergency, my eyes would scan the room. I saw patients and visitors, who were mostly very worried people. Interspersed with them were the doctors and staff, who were always very busy people. But in one corner would be Rita, an island of quietness, utterly different from all of them.

Working at my new job, my emotions kept pulling me away to India, and I could hardly wait to rush out of the building to call home at night, but the new job thrilled me all the same. Patients who came to this clinic had either very rare diseases or very full wallets. My instructions were to be very gentle with all of them. I had landed myself in the hospital equivalent of the most expensive and exclusive French restaurant, but serious medicine, the highest caliber of medicine in fact, was being practiced. My love of learning quickened, and I poured new skill into my hands.

I also quickly discovered the tricky business of telling sickness from health.

One of my first revelations of this came early. I was told to work up a physical on a prominent man who routinely came to the clinic once a year. He was due in at five that afternoon, but by nine o'clock I was still waiting, quite unhappy. I had missed calling Rita by four hours. At last I was told that he was in his room. It was one of the nicest rooms, and a prominent decoration in it was a bouquet of flowers with greetings from President Nixon. As I walked down the hall, I could hear loud wheezing. It sounded very alarming to me, so I rushed into the room. What I saw appalled me.

The man was enormous. He weighed at least 250 if not 300 pounds. His feet were grotesquely swollen. His puffy red face gave out gasps with every breath. He apologized for being late, but his jet had had to be refurbished. He had barely enough time to get here after delivering the commencement address at a huge state university in the South. I didn't know anything about a life like his, nothing about vital, all-night negotiations or what it meant to control millions of votes, which they said he did, but as I took his medical history, it was clear that I was seeing a seriously sick man.

He worked twenty hours a day, he proudly informed me. For years, his habit had been to smoke three packs of cigarettes a day. Since he liked Scotch, he allowed himself to drink it whenever he wanted. At present, he put back a bottle and a half every day. When I examined him, I discovered — no great surprise — that he had advanced cirrhosis of the liver and several of the complications that accompany gross overweight. I asked him how he felt.

"Great," he shot back. "Never felt better. Never get sick, either."

"Really?" I said in amazement.

He looked at me a little more closely. "You know, I just come here every year for my checkup, just to make sure I'm still okay. I am, aren't I?"

I got out of there somehow and went to consult my attending physician.

"My God, you didn't say anything to him, did you?" he asked.

I said that I didn't know what to tell him. Naturally, I thought he should immediately stop drinking and smoking. If he stayed in the clinic on a monitored diet, we might be able to reverse some of his damaged functions as his weight came down. The liver, of course, would not regenerate.

My chief didn't pause. "Don't tell him anything like that. He'll go into DTs if we take away his Scotch. He's been living this way for forty years. Who knows what keeps him going? We don't. He is extremely powerful, and if he got this far, it's ridiculous to change him until he at least realizes that there is something wrong. Remember," he said as I left, "you must be gentle with these patients."

The attending physician knew what he was talking about. Whenever we told patients that they should mend their ways — stop drinking, quit smoking, lose 40 pounds, get off sleeping pills and Valium — they looked very unhappy. They were what they were, and they didn't want to change. We felt very frustrated. We knew what was good for these people, but we were pouring water into broken pots. Every day we also saw patients — most of them women, not young — who came to us complaining of weakness and loss of energy. For many of them this had become a way of life. They felt vaguely depressed all the time. Most of them were overweight. The only difference between them and the patients seen in every doctor's office was that some of these women came from the richest families in America.

They showed up on the doorstep of this prestigious clinic

because it was famous for treating extremely rare diseases. It was one of the main reasons that top doctors joined the staff. For any doctor who had fallen in love with a rare diagnosis, this was a perfect place to observe fascinating syndromes that one never runs across in general practice. Since treatments were often of the utmost delicacy, there were only a handful of places in the country that could offer care like ours.

The bulk of our patients, ninety-nine out of a hundred, did not suffer from such disorders. But many hoped they did. My own field of endocrinology was ripe for this, since the common symptoms of insomnia, lassitude, and obesity can be (but almost never are) indications of underlying pathologies, such as tumor of the pituitary or the pancreas. I therefore saw my share of female patients who lived on the fantasy that they had "a gland problem." Perhaps they had even been right in their nightmares all along — it was cancer.

I was discovering the other side of the story from the physician who grows into the habit of seeing his patients as diseases. These women longed to be seen as diseases. They were suffering the dread of having no name for what was wrong with them. If we said that what was wrong didn't have a name, they felt let down, even cheated. They were paying thousands of dollars to be told that they were sick. If only they could be correctly diagnosed, then the responsibility for making them well shifted to their doctors. Being told that they were not victims of a disease meant that they were on their own again.

I became so tense about their reactions that I developed a little rap for them. As soon as I walked into the room, I would say, "Great news! You don't have hypoglycemia. You don't have hypothyroidism. Your pituitary is not out of whack. And your endocrine profile conclusively proves that you don't have cancer of the pancreas. You are very lucky."

This subterfuge might have helped my nerves a little, but the patients knew I was telling them the worst: they were well. They looked back at me unhappily, and their faces fell. We both knew they needed a solution, but standard American medicine did not extend one to them. They came to us because they believed in the system, but the system wasn't letting them in.

Many people now say that the system of American medicine needs improvement and perhaps drastic overhauling. But what is "the system"? After two years in America, I thought I knew the answer. The system consists of thousands of hospitals and hundreds of thousands of doctors. Within this system there is endless activity, developing medical knowledge and giving rise to new drugs, new surgery, new equipment. Billions of dollars are spent on it, with no end to the spiral of increasing costs. The president of General Motors has pointed out that GM already pays more for the health care of a worker than for the steel that goes into the car he is building. But is that the system?

Now I don't think so. All of those things are like a mammoth beehive, built up of one tiny cell repeated millions and millions of times. If you break it down into its basic unit, the medical system is just a doctor and a patient, just two people. When they meet, they have a personal exchange, with the doctor playing one part and the patient the other. If the exchange turns out well, you have the practice of medicine. If it turns out badly, you have problems. Either way, the system is basically simple, because doctor and patient, the unit of the system, don't change that much from year to year or from country to country.

So if I ask myself, "How am I going to improve the system?" I really am asking only about two people. All that needs to be done is to have them play their parts well. In the present scheme of things, that may be a lot to ask. Patients who want to be seen as diseases all too often find doctors who will oblige them. It takes both sides to keep the cycle of disease and cure going, but I think the primary responsibility lies with the doctors. Recently I heard a story about one doctor who grew sick of seeing his patients as diseases. He analyzed, correctly I think, that his training from its outset had narrowed his conception of health care. Medical school is predominantly disease-oriented, and students spend many hours learning about the most minute indications of unusual pathologies. The entire cycle of disease and cure is strongly reinforced every day thereafter in the small, highly controlled world of the doctor's office.

This doctor saw that he had grown with time to look at his patients, not as people, but as walking syndromes. When he opened the door of his waiting room, there weren't three people waiting for him, but one chronic renal failure, an adult-onset diabetes, and a post-infarct angina pectoris. He decided that he didn't want to face another morning of this gray affliction.

His deeper reason for wanting to change was that he felt his view of patients as diseases was not productive. Looking at his case load, he saw that only about 20 percent of his patients with serious disease, such as a malignancy, responded to treatment believing that their doctor could do them any good. With these 20 percent he could expect a measure of success. Well-being was likely to return, and some would be successfully remitted. A scattering would even enjoy remarkable total recoveries. They would not permit their disease to triumph.

The remaining patient load, far and away the majority, responded to him with dread — sometimes openly, most of the time furtively. It was the same dread surrounding their whole sickness. They regarded their situation with fear and hopelessness. Although as physician he played the part of curer, his treatments lacked that all-important ingredient, the patient's confidence in his own strength to recover.

So this doctor drew the inevitable conclusion that he was

not really doing his job, curing disease. He looked inside himself and discovered, in a moment of exceptional clarity, that maybe he was keeping his patients sick. By seeing them as diseases, perhaps he was fostering a diseased system and beyond that a diseased world, with himself at the center. Like a spider in its web, he gave off something sticky that entrapped his patients. Many physicians have gotten this far in their thinking, but they don't see how they can change the system.

This doctor knew that he was right. Once he had stopped barreling full-throttle down the track of standard medicine, he had noticed signs pointing in other directions. All sorts of alternative medicine existed off the main track, and because he had a terrifically fast mind that could go after new treatments like a wolf after rabbits, he learned a lot in a short period of time. He knew that he had much more to offer his patients as people than he ever did when he saw them as diseases.

So this physician decided to take a positive step. He sat down and wrote a letter to all his patients and said something like this:

> I want you all to be perfectly healthy. Come to me now, while you are well, and let's discuss together how we can preserve your health. Don't look at me as an authority who has magic powers. Don't depend on me to be the mechanic for fixing your damaged bodies. I have changed.
>
> I regard you all as intimately connected with me in the workings of the entire universe. Together we can discover the perfect healer within each of you. I don't want to be a mechanic anymore. I don't want you to fear me. Share your lives with me, and we can put an end to this terrible inheritance of disease that makes our lives so threatening. Peace.

Soon he got responses to his letter. For every hundred he had sent out, about twenty patients answered. They were the same 20 percent who knew how to get well in the first place.

He went on to have great experiences with them, teaching them about inner healing and holistic medicine, but he hadn't really changed the system.

I think I know why the 80 percent who did not respond were not able to benefit: insight couldn't help them when it was another person's insight. A great teacher has called this the tragedy of knowledge. No matter how much water pours from a spring, it can't be carried away in broken pots. A doctor cannot make patients well by telling them the glories of wholeness and health.

At the same time, wholeness and health are obviously the way. The current system has gone so far in the other direction, concentrating on disease and cure, that a vacuum has been created. The basic unit of doctor and patient is not working smoothly. The common idea in America is that medical technology solves problems. Inside the system, however, doctors realize that this is a perilous belief. But there is so much momentum in the system that doctors go with it, telling themselves that, after all, progress is always being made.

They will continue to tell themselves so even if the medical statistics often say something quite different. Thousands of heart bypass grafts, for example, are performed by surgeons every year. There is even a certain glamour about them. Perhaps a celebrity or executive has clogged his coronary arteries with calcified fat and therefore starved his heart muscle for oxygen. A heart attack is imminent. He is rushed to a world-famous hospital, where he is placed under the knife of a world-famous surgeon to have the bypass graft. It is duly recognized in the newspapers: a success.

Recurrent stabbing pain in the chest, which is a late symptom of coronary artery disease, can be terrifying. The afflicted patients feel that warnings are shooting their way directly from Fate. No wonder that the "miracle" surgery is famous. No wonder the patients want to go home free of pain and never think about their diseased hearts again. Yet the long-term statistics inform us that this expensive procedure, which inflicts considerable trauma upon the body, shows very little success at prolonging life expectancy. People with grafts will suffer from heart disease again. And it remains the number one killer in the country. Some doctors would say that the bypass graft has not been a success at all. You'll have to wait for a new miracle tomorrow.

Looking at the situation, one might easily despair. There is no surgery devoid of trauma. There are no drugs without side effects. Yet our system is made up almost entirely of drugs and surgery. What can be done? How can we restore the basic unit of medicine — one doctor making contact with one patient — to a healthy state?

We first of all should *want* to be well in a great way. Otherwise, our problems will always be greater. Health should be not simply strong but invincible. It should be so perfect that nothing better can be imagined and nothing worse can touch it. "Give me health and a day and I will make the pomp of emperors ridiculous." This comes from Ralph Waldo Emerson, who aimed for exuberant vitality in everything. No one else has made normal well-being seem quite so godlike: "The universe is the property of every individual in it. It is his, if he will. He may divest himself of it; he may creep into a corner and abdicate his kingdom, as most men do, but he is entitled to the world by his constitution."

The constitution of man, his mind and body, tunes him to the universe and gives him title to it. If Emerson is right in this, then we had better start looking more closely at what it takes to assume our rightful possession: it takes health. Only that. But perfect health, pure and invincible, is the state we have lost. Regain it, and we regain a world.

Emerson reminds us not to be small. Whenever I read him, I feel the sun radiating from a soul. I am entertaining a wandering lord, hearty and sunburned, who has brought me news of a warm, vital land. Over that land he holds sway as absolute ruler. There, one always rises to greet the same serene conditions — "health and a day." That wholesome place is included in the healthy mind and body of Emerson the man, and while he keeps company with me, I can believe I am a titan: "A man is a god in ruins. When men are innocent, life shall be longer, and shall pass into the immortal as gently as we awake from dreams."

It has been a long time since such thoughts were prized, however. Wake up to immortality? No, there have been too many wars, too much sickness, too many heaps of disillusion. Eventually a perfectly healthy man like Emerson came to be dismissed as an optimist. Emerson does try to cheer people up, but more than that, he is trying to give them back their birthright. He is motivated by his own healthiness, which has banished weakness and made room for compassion.

In India, there are images of saints so perfect in their spirits that they are ready to walk across the threshold into higher worlds. But as they leave, they cannot help but look backward to extend a hand. That is how they are pictured — halfway stepping into Heaven but halfway beckoning to other men over their shoulders. They want us to come with them; they feel compassion.

Perhaps only a few have crossed over the threshold to become angelic doctors, but their actions and words tell the rest of us what to do. People have been told to live with a high ideal in mind and not to fritter their days away in petty whirlwinds. The course of love and compassion has been laid out clearly over and over again. Above all, the true healers have said that life must be natural.

Bringing medicine back to a more natural condition is important. The basic unit of medicine is natural, after all — a person in trouble seeking help from someone who knows the cure. Leaving medical technology aside, this relationship will always be best when it is simplest and therefore most natural.

A story is told about Charaka, the greatest exponent of Ayurveda, who wanted a position as physician to the king. He presented himself at court and asked for the appointment.

"But I already have a hundred physicians," the king replied. "Why would I want another one?"

"You need only one in the first place," Charaka retorted, "if he knows more about medicine than the hundred." Charaka then challenged the hundred court physicians to pose questions to him. If he answered all of them correctly, then he in turn would ask them only one question, which he did not believe all their knowledge put together could answer. The royal vaidyas were angry at Charaka's audacity, so they asked him question after question about anatomy, pathology, herbs, diet, surgery. Finally, there was nothing more to ask. Charaka knew everything about Ayurveda that they did. Then Charaka asked his one question.

"What two medicines," he asked, "are good for all diseases, can be prescribed to every man in every time and place, and cost nothing?" The royal vaidyas had no reply, because they had already exposed everything they knew. The answer, declared Charaka, is simple: a walk in the early morning and sunlight.

The tale records that the king was so delighted with this answer that he fired his hundred physicians and hired Charaka on the spot. He was a wise king. Any doctor who points the way to nature has found the source of health. Sunshine and a walk in the early morning may seem like primitive remedies to us, but perhaps that shows how far we have to go toward becoming gods.

Our progress toward perfect health can assert itself even among the ruins. The choice to evolve and go forward can always take hold, and deeper urges, such as love and hope, begin to exert a force. Once a man takes a step for love, he wants to take a second; eventually he will scale the alps of his heart. "We are never tired, so long as we can see far enough." Emerson again.

I spent two years at the prestigious clinic, happy to further my career. I still burned to get ahead, and as much as the next man I was in love with a rare diagnosis. Endocrinology posed a tremendous intellectual challenge from the start. Another phase of my life was beginning at the same time. Within three days of starting on the job, I received the most joyous news. Rita had had our baby in India.

A month later I chugged down to New York, having bought my own VW bug. I seemed to pace the airport forever until I saw my wife walking toward me, carrying only a basket. I looked inside and saw a tiny, tiny head, two hands, two twinkling feet. My daughter, my Mallika. She probably wasn't going to be president of the United States. I gazed for a while, then I took Rita very tenderly into my arms.

7

The Glass Mountain

DURING the middle and late seventies, I was preoccupied with building my own private practice in Boston. My patient load grew larger and larger, and in time I became affiliated with half a dozen hospitals. I knew that my medical antecedents were exotic in certain ways, but that was well suppressed. In my own mind, I had joined the mainstream of modern medicine. My ambition was to equal or surpass my American colleagues.

A few years later, the *Boston Globe* ran an article criticizing the influx of doctors trained abroad who had immigrated to the United States to take advantage of the rewards of practicing medicine here. Doctors trained in America felt threatened by the competition, and they resented it that foreign doctors could be licensed here so easily.

I did not feel personally implicated in this squabble, however, and I might have let it blow over quietly. I did not see the standards of American medical practice crumbling. But one implication did offend me: that any doctor who went to school abroad must automatically be inferior in his knowledge and skill. I wrote a heated objection to the newspaper.

In a few days, the health editor called me, interested in my own background. I told him my story, and he sent a photographer out to take my picture. The next week I saw myself on the *Globe*'s front page. I was quoted at length defending my credentials and all but claiming that racial prejudice was involved. A dozen jubilant Indian doctors in the Boston area (most of them my friends) called me up to congratulate me. But my office received three times as many calls from outraged American doctors who were angry that I had broken rank to criticize the profession.

This single incident aside, I felt thoroughly assimilated into Boston medicine. The physicians who objected to foreign-trained competition were looking the wrong way, anyway. A grass-roots protest was building that would be far more threatening to them. It was headed by patients who felt alienated by the drift toward technology which doctors on the whole admired. I had started out treating Indian villagers, who could never have adapted to health care by machine. Naively, I assumed that Americans must be different. Most of them seemed amazingly willing to bend to the system. And those who could not bend managed to be fairly unobtrusive — for a time.

Every patient is really a villager at heart, I believe, lost and afraid when he comes in contact with doctors, but willing to trust in medicine if he feels that his physician cares. If patients feel misused, however, then their shock of disturbance will ripple through all of medicine. And that, of course, is what began to happen. Here are a few stories from my own experience. These patients could not conform to our system, so they broke. They taught me that a new trend had to begin, moving toward simplicity and human contact.

The first was a young woman with asthma. I followed her for about three years, from the time she was twenty-five. Since childhood, she had suffered from mild bronchial asthma, usually not requiring any treatment. Her attacks were almost always brought on by emotional upset. At one point this woman went through a fairly traumatic divorce, and her asthma responded by becoming worse, with more frequent and more severe episodes. She made several trips to my office for treatment. Noticing that she came in upset, I could usually relieve her symptoms simply by placing her in a quiet room and asking her to relax. Sometimes I added a mild bronchial dilator, not much stronger than those she could buy in a drugstore. I also suggested that she learn meditation as a relaxation technique. She was reluctant to agree.

One weekend, when she had a particularly heated argument over the phone with her estranged husband, she felt the onset of an attack. As she became progressively shorter of breath, she called my office. She was told that I could not see her — I was out of town for the day — but if she would wait a few minutes, the covering physician would call her back with some advice. She began to feel panicky, which only made it harder for her to breathe. She decided to drive to the nearest emergency room, about fifteen minutes away.

Unfortunately, an accident had occurred on the highway, causing a traffic jam. The woman's anxiety increased, and her bronchial spasms grew worse. Her breathing was now very labored, coming in fitful, shallow gasps. Her heart began to pound, and she felt so dizzy that she feared losing control of the car. She rummaged desperately through her purse for a pill. A psychiatrist had prescribed some Valium for her during the period of her divorce. The last two were in her purse; she swallowed them both.

They didn't help. The dizziness grew worse, and she began to feel drowsy. With great effort, she finally managed to get to the hospital. Then she passed out in the parking lot. The Valium had obviously depressed her respiratory center and made her condition even worse. Two paramedics discovered her slumped over the wheel of her car. She was unconscious, her face had turned blue, and they could detect very little spontaneous breathing. The intern in the emergency room was fresh out of Harvard Medical School and primed for aggressive intervention.

Five minutes after her arrival, he had measured her arterial blood gases and ordered an intravenous solution with large amounts of antibiotics, bronchodilators, and corticosteroids. It wasn't actually clear which of these drugs she needed, but in an emergency it is standard to use the shotgun approach and hope that something works. He inserted a tube into her lungs and put her on a respirator to enable her to breathe. Then she was transferred to intensive care. When I checked in a day later, she was still on the respirator, but a complication had set in. The tube in her throat had irritated her so much that she had coughed up gastric juice from her stomach and then aspirated it — that is, breathed it into her lungs. As a result, she developed aspiration pneumonia.

An infectious disease consultant was called in, and he prescribed a more powerful, broad-spectrum antibiotic. Another try with the shotgun. In three days, the pneumonia began to clear up. However, because of the patient's general debility, aggravated by high doses of antibiotics combined with the steroids, a life-threatening fungal infection set in, called moniliasis. This frequently develops in people whose immune system has been so drastically compromised. In essence, the drugs the woman was put on had knocked out her pneumonia, but at the cost of knocking out much of the rest of her own immune defenses. She went into septic shock, her blood pressure dropped, and her awareness became feeble and unclear.

More consultants were called in. She was seen by a neurologist because of her worsening mental status, by a nephrologist because of her deteriorating kidney function — this had occurred after her blood pressure dropped — by a pulmonologist because of her worsened lung function, and by a cardiologist because of an irregular heartbeat that resulted from inadequate oxygen in her blood. She underwent electrocardiograms, pulmonary function tests, a brain scan, and electroencephalography. She was tested countlessly for blood gases and daily changes in her body chemistry. She lay in her bed with catheters inserted into her heart, her bladder, her pulmonary blood vessels, and her lungs.

She was finally weaned off the respirator after about two weeks. She felt extremely depressed, so a psychiatrist put her on antidepressants. She was counseled by a social worker, who only increased her anxiety and anger. We tried hard to cut down her medications but to no avail. An asthma attack would flare up every time we decreased even one of the drugs. This woman was finally discharged from the hospital a month after she had arrived. Her bill totaled about $30,000. She is now home on disability. Her medications consist of two bronchodilators, an antidepressant, another aerosol bronchodilator in case of attacks, corticosteroids, multivitamins, and a tranquilizer.

All of these, with the possible exception of the vitamins, cause her to endure multiple side effects, including muscle wasting and osteoporosis, a thinning of the bones. The steroids alone have caused or contributed to numerous conditions: diabetes, abnormal fat distribution, a tendency to bruise easily due to weakened blood vessels, and worsening depression. If the diabetes is not carefully monitored, she looks forward in the long run to developing disease in her kidneys, vascular system, and heart. If the diabetes becomes serious enough, she may go blind.

She no longer considers me her physician because, as she put it when I last saw her, "I need medicine, not advice." She now changes doctors the way most women change dresses. Each one generally gives her a new medicine, usually to offset the adverse effects of the old ones. If this woman is unlucky, she will live only ten or twenty more years, in considerable misery and discomfort. She feels continually hostile and blames everyone she sees — me, her new doctors, her psychiatrist, her former husband, and the social worker.

It is almost too cruel to describe this case, much less to comment on it. The term "iatrogenic disease" was coined for illness brought on by the physician in his attempt to heal. But how well can any phrase denote such suffering? It is a doctor's shame.

Yet every physician in clinical practice has seen such patients. When they come in sick, he does the routine things — a diagnosis, a test, a prescription. They come back sicker. So he steps up their medication and orders a battery of tests. But the new tests and the stronger medication don't help. Nothing helps. For no reason known to Harrison's *Principles*, the illness will not respond, and complications begin to develop, growing worse the harder the physician struggles to find a cure.

At a certain point, the doctor senses the worst. He tells himself that this one is sliding away, like a climber on a glass mountain. His only consolation is to tell himself that, after all, he did the right thing. But the sum total of so many right things was a disaster.

What can doctors do in such cases, considering that they are unpredictable? There are really only two answers: develop more cures or develop fewer cases. My own preference by now should be obvious. Doctors already spend years learning to tell which corticosteroid or antibiotic to prescribe. They can offer patients the miracle of a coronary bypass graft, knowing full well that the last miracle incurred too many problems. It is absolutely certain that in time the current miracle will do the same.

It is just now that we are waking up from a delusion. All medical care is not disease and cure. The reality of disease processes is different, and much simpler, from what older generations thought it was. Disease starts out humbly in the body, as some imperceptible imbalance, and proceeds slowly from there. The outcome of a full-blown disease may be devastating, but it has been built up through insignificant everyday actions. What we eat and drink, how we behave, how our emotions affect us — these are small things. When they support well-being, we don't give them a second thought. But no action is lost on the body. We are always building. Every bite of food, every breath, every thought, is like laying a brick, even if we aren't aware that we are building.

If I could turn back the clock, my young asthma patient would not have reached the point of crisis. She would have been educated from the start about the causes that precipitate her illness. She would have been told that her emotions played a crucial part. Knowing that, she could have relied on breathing exercises, relaxation, and even meditation rather than a squeeze from her plastic bottle of bronchodilator. If she had been reached early, as a child, she would not have been overwhelmed by her attacks. When one began to set in, she would have drunk an herbal tea that acts as a mild bronchodilator but has no side effects and no risk of dependency. She would also have known how to go inward to direct her attention in a therapeutic way. She would have felt confident rather than panicky, which makes a critical difference in asthma. A poised self-control would be her strongest defense.

Her doctor would also have pointed out the daily routines — exercise, rest, sleeping habits — that reduce attacks to a minimum. Added to that would have been a special diet suited to asthmatics. Over time, the diet and the daily routine would have readjusted her physiology and brought it back from the specific imbalance that causes asthma. Her doctor's most important advice, however, would have been that she was responsible for her own condition. She could choose the affirming attitudes that promote health. She could live without fear.

By turning back the clock, I am giving this woman a different existence. But I would also have to orient her to a different medicine. Doctors do not know asthma from the side of well-being, only from the side of disease. The herbs, daily routine, exercises, meditation, and diet I describe do not exist in modern medicine. They do exist in Ayurveda. That is one of its great contributions. It gives a patient control over himself long before he becomes a patient.

The second story concerns a man in his forties, a Boston fireman. I first saw him in the emergency room of a suburban hospital, where he had come with sudden and severe chest pain. While I was examining him, he told me that the pains had started quite recently. They were bad enough to convince him that he had a heart condition. I told him that he should withhold judgment until we went through a complete checkup, but he insisted that he knew what was wrong. Moreover, he wanted to retire with disability. At the end of the exam and after asking him a series of questions to determine the exact nature of his pain, I informed him that in my opinion he did not have heart disease. He was not reassured, however, and left in low spirits.

Two nights later he was back with the same complaint, only now the pain was worse and came more often. The emergency room physician could find nothing wrong by listening to his heart. When I was called in to consult, I saw that the patient looked anxious and definitely had developed severe pain, but I, too, found no irregularity in his heart. He insisted once again that he had a heart condition and wanted to retire on disability. I did not necessarily mean to be skeptical, but our area of Massachusetts offers a very generous pension, up to full salary for life, to policemen and firemen who retire because of heart disease.

Now the man became a regular in the emergency room. He always showed up late at night and always had the same story. I decided to send him for an echo cardiogram, a very sophisticated test of cardiac function. The results came back completely normal. Still he returned, and over time he became more and more anxious. I sent him for angiography to determine if his coronary arteries were blocked. Once again, the tests were negative. However, this patient became so obviously distraught that after many sessions I agreed to write a doctor's report declaring that he should retire with disability from the force because of recurrent chest pain.

In a few weeks, his case came up for review before a board of examiners. I went in to appear as his recommending physician. I stated, before three other doctors, one of them a cardiologist, my reasons for considering my patient disabled. The cardiologist asked me if I had detected any abnormality in the structure or function of this man's heart. I said that I had not: the tests were always normal. The board very quickly decided to refuse disability. When I broke the news to him, my patient became very upset. He went home immediately.

Two nights later I was called down to the emergency room. My fireman again, I thought, right on schedule. Except that this time was different: he had suffered a massive heart attack. At least 90 percent of the heart muscle had been destroyed or seriously damaged. I walked over to the man, who was stretched out on a litter in the hallway, wondering what I could possibly do. He had enough strength to open his eyes and recognize me. He whispered, "Now do you believe me?" Then he died.

What a patient believes can be the deciding factor in his disease. This is not surprising, given that his own ability to recover is always primary; everything the physician does, including the most advanced surgery or the most powerful drugs, is secondary. A great deal of credit goes to the art of medicine which should go to the art of belief. Miracle operations come and go, but belief has endured forever.

Before the heart bypass graft became the preferred surgery

for heart disease, there had been good success with an earlier procedure called an intramammary implant. The way it worked is this: one of the arteries that feeds blood to the breasts, the intramammary artery, was located. The surgeon fished it around until he had curved it back toward the heart. Then he sewed it in a position so that it fed blood to the heart in place of the coronary arteries, which were clogged. The procedure is serious. It involves cracking open the rib cage at the breastbone and exposing the heart to the air. Only patients with advanced heart disease underwent it. And they did better for quite a while. Their severe pains decreased or disappeared entirely.

Then a smart cardiologist had the notion to take angiograms of the heart vessels soon after surgery. The pictures showed that the intramammary arteries blocked up with plaque very soon after the patients went home, within a few months. Sometimes it was only a few weeks. Why were a percentage of these patients free from symptoms? No one knew. Then a surgeon decided to perform an intramammary implant without the implant. He simply cracked open the ribs, exposed the heart to view, and then closed the patient up. The results were even more mysterious than before. A certain percentage of patients did just as well, on the average, as the ones who received the real procedure.

Clearly, the power of belief was at work here. Most doctors would admit that, but because medical school has honed their minds to look for concrete findings and prescribe concrete treatments, they are baffled by such phenomena. They want to stick with a confident or "hard" diagnosis, not shadowy guesswork. But nature seems to be playing tricks with this scheme. Yesterday's hard diagnoses are getting softer and softer. Now, almost every disease is believed to be involved with the patient's mind. Still, what people trust is the hardware of medicine — scalpels and drugs, hospitals and apparatus. Who wants to lean on so slender a reed as mere belief?

Doctors are reluctant to probe into a patient's personal beliefs, but they nevertheless sense them. A senior oncologist, or cancer specialist, at one of the teaching hospitals in Boston told me that he has developed an intuition about patients which enables him to predict their prospects the moment they walk through his door. Every patient who comes to him receives the same professional consideration and is offered the best course of treatment. But, after many years of practice, this doctor has discovered two types of patients, those who respond to their cancer with courage and willingness and those who struggle hopelessly. Even though both groups seem to be equal in their symptoms, it is really like treating two different diseases. One is curable, the other fatal.

Every experienced doctor has seen patients who died of a diagnosis. The body could live with the symptoms, but the mind couldn't live with the bad news. Something in them would not believe in recovery. No physician thinks he is the one who cures. Many would say that the art of medicine begins only after the art of belief. Belief, however, is more or less inaccessible to a doctor. It stands at the center of a person's own values. It is an attribute, like love and compassion, which is closest to the self.

The Boston fireman who died of a heart attack was working directly through his belief about being sick. His thoughts were able to trigger substances in the body that are subtle and yet potent. And the subtlest changes are just the ones that can be the most powerful. The amount of adrenaline it takes to make you jump away from a snake on the path is extremely minute: it would sit comfortably in a little droplet on the head of a pin. When the Ayurvedic texts prescribe delicate measures for a disease — a few herbs, a carefully modified diet — it is because they want the action to be subtle. They are heading directly to the level of physiological functioning that is most powerful. These measures do not necessarily work to combat full-blown diseases, but the answer here, as with my asthma patient, is to start the treatment before the critical stage.

I once had a middle-aged patient who was in the advanced stages of lung cancer. One of his worst symptoms was pleural effusion; that is, his chest cavity filled with water that seeped out of the lung tissue. Whenever this occurred, he found it nearly impossible to breathe. He had had three or four such episodes in the space of a few months. Every time, he was rushed to an emergency room, where a tube was inserted into his chest. He was placed on oxygen through a respirator while the fluid was drawn out through a needle inserted into the chest. The whole procedure was miserable for him, and he grew very anxious whenever it needed to be done.

Recently he began to respond to treatment quite well. Then he woke up one night feeling smothered and sensed that another episode was about to begin. His daughter phoned me in a panic. I ordered an ambulance and called ahead to the emergency room to notify them that he was coming. I asked the emergency room doctor to take an X-ray to determine if fluid effusion was the cause of the patient's shortness of breath. In half an hour he called back, told me that the X-ray showed a large, shadowy mass, and advised me that he was going to start emergency procedures to drain the lung. I asked if he was sure that the shadow was fluid. He sounded irritated. The patient had lung cancer. What else could it be?

I told him to wait for a few minutes until I arrived. At the hospital, I found my patient checked into a room and breathing through an oxygen mask. His eyes had a look of wild fear in them. He sat up for me; I took the mask away and asked him to meditate for five minutes. (I knew at first hand that he had practiced meditation in the past.) He agreed. Ten minutes later he opened his eyes. It was obvious to both of us that he was breathing normally. In fact, considering his condition, his breathing sounded remarkably calm and regular. There was no fear in his eyes. He slept well all night after I left him. One can't help but think of all the equipment that lay unused in the emergency room that night.

The more I see incidents like this, the more I am convinced that the art of belief is indispensable. There is really no such thing as the absence of belief. But there are tall hedges around *right* belief, and the tallest may be conventional medicine itself.

One of my friends is a Pakistani doctor named Simon. He is about my age, highly respected in his research-oriented field, and an aggressive tennis player. He called me to say that he had been experiencing chest pains. At first they were mild, but now they were quite sharp and located directly over his heart.

Simon began to worry. He underwent a routine electrocardiogram, but the results were ambiguous. An abnormality had showed up in one of the leads. I reminded him that eleven leads are used in the test. It was likely that his heartbeat was simply exhibiting a normal variation. He did not sound very reassured when he hung up.

The next time Simon called, he had been to a cardiologist. He was advised to have a stress test, which is a nearly conclusive measure of coronary artery disease. During the test, the patient walks on a treadmill until his heartbeat becomes quite high. In Simon's case, it went from 80 beats a minute to 180. He felt no pain. Indeed, he never felt chest pain while he was playing tennis, either. As soon as his heartbeat was elevated, Simon was injected with radioactive thallium. This is used because it shows up well on the scanning monitor. After the thallium reached his heart, pictures were taken to determine if the coronary arteries were open or closed. Open arteries are healthy; closed ones are characteristically blocked with plaque, deposits of calcified fat. Such arteries are the cause of coronary artery disease.

Simon told me that his left coronary artery had showed up larger than his right one on the thallium scan, suggesting that there might be a defect in one of the branches of the right coronary artery. His cardiologist therefore advised him that he might have heart disease. To resolve any doubts, he should have a coronary angiogram. Cardiologists call this the gold standard for detecting coronary artery disease. Simon kept thinking of Arthur Ashe, he said. Ashe was playing championship tennis until the day he had a heart attack.

I told Simon that nothing he had said so far made me think that he had coronary artery disease. He asked if he could bring me his EKG and thallium scan. When I looked at them, I was more sure than ever that his heart was absolutely normal. An irregular heartbeat and differences in the size of the coronary arteries are not certain signs of heart disease.

I asked Simon to show me where his pain occurred. He placed his fingers over his left breast. I asked if the pain was sharp or dull. Very sharp. I asked if it came when he was resting. Only then. In that case, I pointed out, he almost certainly did not have heart disease. The characteristic pain from heart disease comes right in back of the sternum, in the center of the chest. It is usually dull, and it almost always arises during exercise. In my opinion, there was no need for an angiogram.

The next time I saw Simon was at a party. He pulled me aside and mentioned that his cardiologist happened to be there, too. He was a Pakistani whose name in his native tongue means "devoted to the Lord." He was eminent in his field and an associate of one of the best hospitals in Boston. Would I talk to him? Sure. Simon led me to the porch. I actually felt reluctant to approach his doctor, but Simon insisted. He slumped in a chair while the other doctor and I discussed his case.

"I don't think Simon should have this angiogram," I said.

"Why not?" the cardiologist asked. "He has an abnormality in his EKG. His thallium scan is suspicious. He should have the test."

"Those could be normal variations," I said.

"Don't confuse him." The cardiologist's tone turned a bit sharper. "He needs angiography."

There is a bridge across the river between Cambridge and Boston called the Paul Dudley White Bridge, named for the most famous cardiologist of his time. He treated presidents and royalty. His colleagues called him the king of hearts. In his day, about thirty years ago, coronary angiography did not exist. The thallium scan did not exist. Dr. White would listen carefully to a patient's story, ask him the same questions I had been taught to ask, and then pronounce his diagnosis. On the strength of what Simon had already told me, Paul Dudley White would have sent him home a happy man. He did not have heart disease.

I did not say a word of this to the cardiologist. I mentioned that if Simon was worried, he should consider a few changes in diet and exercise. He might even take up meditation as a relaxation technique.

The cardiologist looked straight at Simon.

"Listen," he said. "You can take up a crank vegetarian diet, go walking three miles every day, and learn something called meditation. But if you want to lead a normal life and play tennis, have the angiogram."

Simon slumped down farther in his chair. His face looked pained. He wanted to lead a normal life and to play tennis.

"But his heartbeat went from 80 to 180 without any pain at all," I shot back. But now I had gone too far.

"Do you know everything about heart disease?" the cardiologist said angrily. "I don't. Simon has put me on the spot. Should he play tennis or shouldn't he? What do you want me to say? He could drop dead on the court tomorrow. He should have the test."

Other doctors in the room started to warm up. Each one had a favorite story, but all with the same gist. A patient who had no sign whatever of coronary artery disease died playing tennis, or golf, or picking up a lampshade. Simon listened very closely.

He seemed like a changed man the next time he called me. He was very embarrassed, but he had to talk to me. His test was coming up the next day. He wondered if afterward he should rely on medicine — he mentioned some of the most powerful drugs for heart disease — or should he plunge in and have a bypass graft?

I told him that he didn't have coronary artery disease.

"But what if I have a fixed lesion?" he asked. A fixed lesion means that the arteries are permanently constricted or blocked in one place; they usually require surgery to be corrected.

I told him that he didn't have a fixed lesion, either. He didn't have any disease, I thought; he was suffering from unreality. He was producing his own drama of disease. But I couldn't say that to a friend. I didn't know what was causing his chest pain, but if he ever found a way to wake up from this scene, he would be all right. I listened for a while, offering some sort of reassurance; then Simon hung up, very disappointed.

I thought about how the angiogram would affect him. In this test an incision is made in the thigh to expose the femoral artery. A catheter is inserted and worked up the blood vessels, past the junction with the aorta, and all the way into the coronary arteries that feed the heart. Then an iodinated dye is injected directly into these arteries, and the monitor shows quite definitely whether there is any blockage. Angiography is relatively safe, much safer than exploratory surgery, but it still involves invading the body. In the mind-body system, it is registered as an important event. You are in a hospital. The full apparatus of medical technology is being brought down, making the patient at the very least feel helplessly dependent and frail. I could see Simon, himself a physician, reading the monitor as it produced its verdict.

After another day or two, Simon called me for the last time.

His voice sounded elated. The angiogram had shown that his arteries were clean. He didn't have heart disease. What is more, the chest pain was completely gone. It was a moment of tremendous relief for both of us. I congratulated him, feeling the same triumphant emotions that come with a real cure. Simon was not going to slide down the mountain after all. Something inside him had held firm; the crisis of unreality had passed.

8

Pacemaker

IF YOU EXPECT TO MEET a citizen of the cosmos, you have to walk through some strange neighborhoods. I stayed seated in the cab of a scooter rickshaw while my friend Farouk got out to talk to the driver in Hindi. We had been putt-putting through Nizammudin, a sector of New Delhi, for half an hour. It is primarily a Moslem part of the city, and very old. All around us we saw minarets and mausoleums where Moghul lords and ladies of three centuries ago are lying, turned to powder. The streets are faring about the same. As we went along, the main roads of Nizammudin had turned into crumbling, crooked lanes and then into gullies that barely passed for streets. What lay ahead of us now were just gullies, pure and simple. The driver halted and shook his head.

"Rickshaw wallah stop here — you walk." Farouk got out and put up a fuss, feebly, but then he came back to fetch me. He smiled.

"Don't worry," he said, "it's not too far, and you'll be amazed when you get there. You'll thank me for the rest of your life."

Perhaps. I had not been back to Delhi for a while now. It

was 1981, and when I stepped off the plane, the heat seemed unbearable. Getting off the plane in summer is like turning into a tandoori chicken, and I hate it. The tandoor is a local type of clay oven which is fired so hot that as soon as a scrawny Indian chicken is thrust in, it roasts almost immediately. The chicken comes out bright pink, like the tender Americans when they step off the plane in summer. So the comparison is not bad.

Our scooter putt-putted away, trailing fumes while Farouk and I negotiated the nearest ravine. It ran like all the other ones, higgledly-piggledy into a chaotic group of houses, mosques, and tombs. We talked about meditation along the way, watched where we were stepping, and ignored the cows.

Farouk thoroughly understands meditation, an interest I had just picked up. He talks about it in terms of quantum physics and chemistry and depth psychology, in the modern way. But he has a soul of light. He also has a religion, which is not a requirement for meditation. Farouk is a Parsi, one of a devout sect in India which began in Persia hundreds of generations ago. Its great prophet is Zoroaster, and its three most famous adherents, in the Western view, are the magi who followed the star to Bethlehem.

Farouk greatly interests me. He has a wonderful mind. He went to England to be trained in the law, did brilliantly there, and on his return home became counsel to the Supreme Court of India. (My accent does not have a British finish, so Farouk seems quite the proper gentleman to me. When I am around him, I tend to remind myself that one should certainly polish one's shoes more than twice a year.) But soon after he was called to the bar, he gave it all up to devote himself to meditation. I must make it clear that he was not renouncing the world. In his view, he was going for a promotion. Meditation is a means to become fully awake. There is a famous Sanskrit verse which says that all the hymns of the Veda come to him who is awake. Since the sacred books of the Veda are said to contain everything, "all the hymns of the Veda" means all the knowledge in the universe. So you see what Farouk meant by a promotion.

I did not know meditation inside out the way Farouk did. But we agreed about it, even then, before I knew the major role it was soon to play in my life. I was sometimes unnerved to visit Farouk on my trips back home. He wakes up and sits in full lotus on the floor of his room. He is dressed in a loincloth with a sacred thread draped across his chest. That in itself would not unnerve me. It is quite common in India. But Farouk emits eerie howls in a loud, shrill voice for most of the morning. Very loud. It is his chanting of Parsi verses. To a non-Parsi, which includes the lion's share of humanity, his chants are so piercing that they make New Delhi cats sound almost melodious. He occupies a little room in Noida, an arid plain outside Delhi where the epic battle recorded in the *Bhagavad-Gita* took place. It is serenely peaceful there now. Sunday at Noida is a good day for Farouk, because he can chant all morning if he likes. His neighbors hate it.

This day, Farouk was quite excited when I showed up. He wanted me to meet with someone of great renown, said to be the preeminent living Ayurvedic physician. His name was Dr. Brihaspati Dev Triguna, and he was the head of the all-India council for Ayurvedic doctors. Three hundred and fifty thousand physicians looked up to this council from the length and breadth of India. A great sage had even called Dr. Triguna the living incarnation of Ayurveda. This was not taken as simply a flowery embellishment. Trigunaji's great specialty was to gain a full diagnosis of his patients simply by feeling their pulse.

"He only has to put three fingers on your wrist," Farouk told me, "and he knows your whole medical history — past, present, and future. It is called *nadi vigyan*, a very ancient art, and he is a master of it. We must go see him. Besides, he's free."

We didn't walk for long before we came to the end of an empty alley. Farouk guided me through a doorway. Here, he told me, is Triguna's waiting room. It was a whole courtyard. We had hardly seen two people in half an hour, and suddenly here, gathered in this open place, were fifty. The crowd seemed to be mostly peasant farmers, Hindus mixed with Moslems, the men in turbans, squatting on the ground under the sun. Many of them sat with tiffin carriers to hold the meals they had brought with them. Some of the children were playing, some were crying, a few were being nursed at the breast.

Farouk and I made our way toward a small building at the end of the courtyard. I could see the tops of minarets over the wall against the hot sky. As I looked around, I noticed a few Westerners in the crowd. Most of them had taken shelter in the area covered with a tin roof. They all sat with bundles of papers in their laps.

Farouk noticed them, too. "You can pick out the Americans. They come with their CAT scan readouts."

"We can't just go in past them," I protested.

"Come on. I know Triguna. He loves to see Western doctors."

We entered the small building and found ourselves in a cool room with green carpets on the floor. The walls had marble insets and inscriptions from Charaka, the greatest ancient authority on Ayurveda. In the middle of the room was a desk and behind it a low divan, where Dr. Triguna sat. I had time to look at him, because he was diagnosing a woman as we entered. She was in *purdah*, which means that one edge of her sari was drawn across her face as a veil so that men would not set eyes on her.

The interview began with her putting out her hand. Dr. Triguna touched her wrist for a few seconds.

"You are *vata dosha*," he told her. This meant that he had determined her general body type. It is a main feature of the diagnosis. *Vata* types are considered quick and thin and prone to fear, among many other characteristics.

"You have unhealthy feelings inside," he went on, "and they are making your body sick." His voice rumbled out from a wrestler's chest. The woman leaned forward intently. "You feel butterflies in the stomach at times. Sometimes knots. You do not get to sleep on time because you worry in bed. Problems moving the bowels."

He took his hand away and fixed her with a look.

"Eat more slowly and make good food for your husband. Be more loving. Your husband is nursing unhealthy emotions, and that is what you are feeling." He then made a few comments on diet and handed her a small slip of paper.

The woman bowed and made the gesture of *namaste* with her hands together. She quickly walked past me. I got the sense that she was extremely impressed by Triguna's advice. She came from an orthodox household, her husband was probably a bricklayer or something, and there were four or five children at home. Such husbands have no time for their wives. They work all day, come home to a late dinner, and then go to bed. The wife was of course unhappy and felt ignored. Dr. Triguna no doubt understood these people well. I didn't see much to it besides that. The prescription he gave her was probably for *brahmi,* I conjectured, a common herb that is said to be relaxing. I considered it the same as telling a patient to drink warm milk before going to bed at night.

By this time I had had a chance to appraise Dr. Triguna. His impressive round bulk was traditionally clothed in white cotton, with a large turban on top. He sat cross-legged on his divan, seeming utterly immovable. He must have been about seventy. He looked the part, I thought, of a bygone king at his audience. He had a great physical presence and the air of sure command. His eyes were sunk in shadowy sockets — they looked knowing. In between his words, which were rather like a lion's cough, the spaces felt very silent.

We walked up to him, and Farouk began to make the introductions.

"I have brought a great man to see you, Trigunaji. He is a

famous doctor in America, one of the most famous. Whatever goes on in the glands of the human body, he knows about it."

What was Farouk doing? I tried to make him stop, but he didn't pay any attention.

"People come from everywhere to the great medical center in Boston where Dr. Chopra is a beacon of wisdom. He is also rich. Rich Americans cannot wait to pay him so that he will make them well. He has studied at the Rockefeller Institute."

My God.

A little more of this, and when I was thoroughly embarrassed, Farouk turned to me and said, "Now let Trigunaji take your pulse."

No, I protested. It was very interesting to see Dr. Triguna at his work, extremely interesting, in fact. I was learning a lot. Maybe Farouk should have his pulse taken. Farouk looked taken aback. It hadn't occurred to me, after all his buildup, that Farouk had not actually allowed Dr. Triguna to diagnose him. So I insisted, and Farouk timidly put forward a bony wrist. Dr. Triguna touched his pulse for a few seconds, then looked hard at Farouk.

"This body no good!" he boomed in English.

All the color drained at once from Farouk's face. He pulled back his arm. Dr. Triguna was now shaking his head mournfully.

"*Vata,*" he intoned, "is very out of balance. You are too thin. You don't eat. You are weak."

I found myself paying attention. The Parsis are a closed group who have bred the same genes, cycle after cycle, for centuries. They do tend toward weak bodies, a high incidence of certain cancers, and thinness. I had always thought Farouk had a starved, sickly body myself. I worried about him physically, but he hadn't taken it to heart.

I could see that Farouk was rapidly losing enthusiasm for his great Trigunaji.

"But you can live a long time if you take care of this body." Triguna kept on with emphatic evenness. "You must eat more slowly. Chew your food and take time to eat. Go to bed on time. Make sure you are rested. Have your meals on time. Sit silently for meditation. Learn to take life more slowly."

Farouk seemed to be cheering up.

"You will live a long, happy life once your body is better," Dr. Triguna ended, and then he gave specific advice about which diet would help Farouk become stronger. His advice seemed simple, but I felt respect for Dr. Triguna. I agreed with what he had said. His words were apt and even profound, when you considered that Farouk's physiology had roots in Parsi bloodlines that went back centuries. Now it was my turn.

Dr. Triguna felt my pulse for a few seconds. He looked down.

"I will tell you," he said. Nothing else.

"Yes?"

"I will tell you," he repeated more slowly. "Later."

"You can't tell me now?" I asked. He shook his head. I thought perhaps Farouk had made him nervous about my incredible importance. I pressed for more. He had my curiosity up now.

"Sometime later," Dr. Triguna insisted. Then, "Maybe a few insignificant things for now." He looked at me shrewdly. It was the real physician's examining look, and very deep.

"Two things," he said. "You think too many unnecessary thoughts. You are always trying to beat a deadline." He made the points come home, somehow. "You have a healthy body, but your life is moving too fast. Thinking too many thoughts leads to high blood pressure. In later life it can cause heart disease."

And what should I do?

"Slow down. There are four important things to gain in life: fame, wealth, a happy family life, and spiritual attainment. You are gaining them all, but too fast. If you get them now, what will you do for the rest of your life? It is important that things come at the proper time. You should sit for five minutes silently before you go to work in the morning. When there is an opportunity, watch a sunset. It is good for your body type. Spend more time with your wife and children. Chew your food slowly. Make sure you move your bowels at the same time every day. Soak seven to ten skinned sweet almonds in a glass of water overnight and eat them in the morning, slowly."

Paper is a cruel critic. When I set Dr. Triguna's advice down on the page, his words may seem naive. To me, they were not. He seemed to *know*. I felt relaxed with him, very relaxed, like water flowing between its banks. He paddled out, tested the currents. Yes, a snag here and there. The water doesn't need to flow so fast or be quite so warm. The river has a long way to run. Take time for it.

He thought for a second and then told me one last thing.

"Ayurveda is very clear about the goal of life. It is to be happy and to receive wise and happy thoughts from every part of the universe."

It was a pivotal moment for me. I felt as if Dr. Triguna read me well, very well. The common things he said as well as the uncommon things wove themselves into a pattern that described me. They seemed at once right and just. I felt that his simplicity of speech was wise. Yes, if I did these things, I would be all right. There was tremendous reassurance here. Dr. Triguna *knew*.

I thanked him shyly. As I got up to leave, I realized that I was deeply affected. I turned and did something that I would have found ridiculous in the West. I gently touched his feet. It was the same gesture of respect I afforded my grandfather when I was a boy. When we were outside, I felt very grateful to Farouk.

"He is as you said," I commented. "He is very good."

Farouk nodded silently, and we walked a little. My senses felt very gently attuned and alert. The hot air of the day had lost its edge. As the twilight drew on, perhaps we would smell the flower I love above all others, Rath-ki-Rani, the queen of the night.

I said a few words, but Farouk kept silent. As we neared the main streets again, he turned to me ruefully.

"Yes," he said, "but this body no good."

I have since then witnessed Dr. Triguna many times and traveled with him to America. I have introduced him in various surroundings — the boardrooms of New York corporations, offices of politicians in Washington, and hospitals in Boston and California. Within a few minutes of his arrival, each room is the same. It has Dr. Triguna in it. He invariably fascinates everyone. Some people listen to my introductory remarks on Ayurveda with barely concealed boredom. So much Indian blah-blah, their faces say.

Then Dr. Triguna places his three fingers on their pulse and starts his lion's mutter while I translate from Hindi into English. He shows right away that he knows these people. "Very good, very healthy bodies in America," he will say, "but very worried minds. People are living too fast, it will make them sick." He does not often feel happy thoughts in the pulse here.

Dr. Triguna seriously tells power brokers that they should move their bowels once a day, and always at the same time. They should chew their food more slowly. They should take soda water with skim milk to bring down their inner fire. It sounds all too easy to dismiss such advice or to think that it was covered in your junior high health class. But Dr. Triguna wins Americans over because they sense that he has peered deeply.

Skeptical Western patients are always asked to write down their medical complaints on paper before the diagnosis, just the ones they want help with. Dr. Triguna touches their wrists, looks very deep with his examining look, and says what he thinks. It is almost always what they have written down. They look impressed. He goes on in his general way, talking about their past and future, their thoughts and motives, so unmedical by our professional standards, but so obviously healthy. And then people really listen.

Dr. Triguna has peered into the whole man. There are not many masters in his school, but there are a billion pupils. All of us sense the whole man when we meet someone else. We may be too timid to admit what we sense or too dull even to notice, but we're undeniably getting a feel. Dr. Triguna has perfected this intuition and made one human instinct a tool of medicine.

I believe he does not even see patients as bodies. They are bundles of consciousness rising to meet him. Something that is just them — a grain, like a seed of them — flows out from their hearts. It makes its way past the snags and eddies of their constitution. It meets with discords and blocks. Then it flows under Dr. Triguna's investigating fingers. Yes, this blood has gone by a bad valve or a bad thought. You like to think about anger. You should tell some jokes and watch the sunset once in a while. His few remarks are the ones you need to hear at the moment, just you among all people and at just this moment among all moments. His patients do not dread him because they feel understood, not simply diagnosed.

Once I presented Dr. Triguna at the office suite of a financier. This man was over seventy-five, in frail health, and very knowledgeable about the East. He understood and loved its deepest concepts. We were shown a room nearby where a fraction of his private art collection was housed, a few highly precious Oriental objects. We sat down at the boardroom table, and I was shown the portrait of the founding father. It was a name all Americans know, although no one knows exactly the size of the fortune.

Dr. Triguna was very polite. He was about seventy-five himself then, and the two men were comfortable together. He took the financier's pulse, made the diagnosis, and gave his opinion — a certain change of diet, certain herbs, some meditation.

"And you should walk to work in the morning," he said in a very definite way.

The financier looked over at me. "I can't do that," he said. It had been years since he had had the time for such a thing, if he ever considered it.

"Play with children every day," Dr. Triguna continued.

"There aren't any children around me."

"The children are in schools. Take candy to the schools and pass it out to them." Dr. Triguna thought for a second. "You are busy. Do it only once a week."

The financier and I burst out laughing at the same time. It sounded so impossible, but absolutely as life should be. Perhaps for a tenth of a second we glimpsed an old man handing out sweets while children loved him. But the crack of light from a sane mind passed. Boardroom portraits cast long shadows.

Dr. Triguna provokes such responses and says such things quite often. He considers the whole man and tries to elevate him, first to normalcy, then beyond. Ayurveda takes the vista of man to be infinite. The universe is the macrocosm, man is the microcosm. But Ayurveda speaks delicately, so delicately that you see Western medicine as clumsy. You see it as using incredibly refined techniques to change only the grossest things. It's as if a man came out from swimming and his doctor had to weigh him on an electronic scale, wait for the water to evaporate from his skin, weigh him again, put the results through computer analysis, and then pronounce his opinion: he is wet. But by now he is not wet anymore.

Dr. Triguna swims with the man instead. One of the most famous fragments of Greek wisdom says, "It is not possible to step into the same river twice." Our bodies are similar, always in motion, much more like rivers than sculptures. Only sculptures stand still. Taking a blood test to the lab is like scraping a little marble dust off the foot of a sculpture. But our bodies don't just stand there waiting. We flow on. Every thought brings a new person into being. It springs up complete with altered biochemistry, a new ebb and flow of enzymes, a new battlefront for the white cells in the blood, and a new freight of oxygen for the hemoglobin in the red cells. All this, billions of changes more than this, with every thought. Nothing is the same even for an instant. If medicine cannot step into the river once, it cannot do it twice.

Ayurveda is nothing if not flow. That is the essence of its intelligence. A man is seen in the moment. He is either young or old. He has a certain body type, of which he is a particular variation. His country and his food are his own and not another man's. The Ayurvedic doctor even looks out the window and considers the time of year and the hour of the day. The herbs he recommends will be different from man to man, country to country, season to season. What is most fascinating, each disease is seen in its own right, and no two diagnoses are ever exactly the same. One man's skin cancer might be curable, another's resistant to treatment, and another's fatal. If the physician's skill is great enough, he knows if a patient will die from a cold.

Dr. Triguna has gathered all of this into his intelligence. It is just Nature he looks at, therefore it is knowable in his nature. He has great learning in herbs, which he mixes and dispenses to his patients as his chief method of actually curing an illness. But he does not rely primarily on his learning or even on cures. He wants to restore the flow. He gives considerable credit to the technology of Western medicine, but he says that it is all in pieces. Where is the whole man in this? Where is the river? We would feel embarrassed to think back on another fragment from the same Greek philosopher, Heraclitus: "Much learning does not teach a man to have intelligence." In Hindi they say, "The learning which is in books, stays in books." Dr. Triguna is not a librarian's doctor.

After spending considerable time with Dr. Triguna and exploring the methods of Ayurveda, I found it possible to explain much of it in our own language. I decided a few years ago that it would be good to set it down. I took a few simple precepts and began to explicate them — I mean the very most basic ideas, such as these: Nature is composed of one intelligence. Man is part of Nature. Therefore, man's intelligence connects him to the universe. It took me an entire book to explain just that. Now I see that one awake doctor is worth much more than all the books. How much is our learning, our gluttony for information, going to teach us? Feel your pulse and reflect.

Dr. Brihaspati Dev Triguna stands out in my life as the master physician. Even if I knew consciously that my condition was perilous, I feel that I would recover under his care. I believe in the goodness of my physician. He told me that the purpose of life is to be happy and to receive wise and happy thoughts from every part of the universe.

I also call him a master at his art as much for what he does not do as what he does. He does not interfere with a patient's life. His fingers merely touch the pace of that life. They sense its rhythms. They extract the knowledge of disharmony, broken vibrations that might cause ill health. It is enough. There is only one healthy pace to Dr. Triguna, the pace of the cosmos. The essence of health is to attend to the pacemaker. Once that is done, disease is done.

9

An Arrow to the Heart

IF WE DIDN'T HURRY, we'd be late at the door of God. Rita and I were praying together, but not to get there any faster. "The door of God" is the literal translation of Haridwar, a city on the Ganges that serves as the gateway to the Himalayas. We had been invited to visit there by my friend Vinod as we were leaving the United States for a trip to India. Now we sat in the back seat of his father's car, alarmed at the driving ability of our Indian chauffeur.

He was weaving crazily down the narrow roads in the manner favored by Indian drivers. The most terrifying part came when we happened to meet a car coming in the other direction. Both cars would head straight at each other until the very last second, and then, as if by telepathy, the drivers swerved halfway into the ditches and passed.

"Faster, faster," Vinod's father implored. Vinod, sitting next to him in the front seat, turned around and beamed. Something very wonderful lay ahead of us, he kept insisting. I found Rita's hand and clutched it. The driver, who had been with the family for years, enthusiastically gunned the engine.

Because we survived, I can thank him now. Our first glimpse

of Haridwar that evening in 1982 was indeed wonderful. The city is a famous pilgrimage site, known to every orthodox believer. Whenever a great *mela,* or festival, is in progress, millions of visitors travel there, and the city is overwhelmed by humanity. It becomes hard to tell the river from the flowing dry Ganges of the streets. But we were creeping up on Haridwar at a quiet time, when it belonged to its inhabitants. As we walked from our car toward the sacred river Ganges, I began to recapture the sensation of being in a holy place, which is a cherished experience to any Indian returning home. The twilight itself seemed like a shrine here. Ahead we began to see the flicker of oil lamps, countless numbers of them, lining a place along the banks called Hari-ki-Podi, the steps to God.

Thousands of people had preceded us there. They stood, palms together, with flowers in their hands, keeping very quiet for such a crowd. Their foreheads were each marked with a spot of holy ashes. We took our places and fell at once into a sense of union with them. *Puja,* the rite of daily devotion, was about to begin. Incense rose around us, and the slow, melodious chanting started.

Indians are bound together by the expression of *puja.* It is performed twice a day, like matins and vespers in the West, but the devotional words are not denominational: they are the words of thanks we took into ourselves simply from hearing our parents in the morning during early childhood. Joining the *puja* at twilight in Haridwar was a reminder to live gladly, put into song. For the moment, I was joining the choir of India and forgetting my single voice. The shadows of the temples lengthened to the horizon and took the day away with them. The swollen green river turned dark in the night and more gentle in its flow, as if accepting our thanks and then rolling over to sleep.

As soon as *puja* ended, a different mood broke out, announced by a sudden eruption of noise. Some boys near me lit fireworks, then babies cried, snake charmers twiddled their flutes, and beggars wailed their pleas. It was suddenly just like the friendly madhouse at the festival *melas*. A thousand people began to dance. The rest passed out sweets or flowers to strangers as whim dictated. I could hear on every side of me women's voices as they took up a favorite *bhajan*, or sacred song. There are hundreds of them, all in praise of life. I wished at that moment that I was a sacred singer, too. We knew that we had to leave, but it was tempting to stay in the midst of such happiness. A city's common devotion had sparked a renewed joy that would last for hours.

We drove out into the country, toward the house of Vinod's grandfather. At that time, the old man was almost ninety. For more than ten years he had been a recluse. He lived alone with one servant and devoted himself to prayers, studies, and meditation. Indians call this *sanyasa*, the time of old age when one lives in silence, not distracted by possessions. Our black Ambassador pulled into a long driveway, and after a quarter of a mile or so we saw a large colonial-style house, more or less a compound, set in lush mango groves. This must be how a rich man takes *sanyasa*, I thought.

In our headlights we caught an unexpected sight: a nearly naked man was sitting in full lotus on the veranda of the house. With quicker eyes, I would have seen that he was wearing a saffron-colored loincloth and beside him lay a walking staff and half a coconut shell. Vinod's reaction to this sight was galvanic. He cried out in joy, leaped out of the car, and ran to prostrate himself at the man's feet. Moving a little more slowly, his father did the same thing. The wandering monk, for that is what he was, came out of meditation. He now looked as excited as the other two, and I could see in his face a look of extraordinary, radiant happiness.

Rita and I came up behind. We felt out of place, but since Vinod and his father had led the way, we also prostrated ourselves before this man. They kept calling him Swamiji, over and over, and in a few minutes I gathered who he was.

He was a seeker, well known to their family, who after many years away had made himself at home for the night. All he owned was the cloth he wrapped around himself, his stick, and his coconut shell. Nothing else in the world — family, home, temple, goods — was his, not even a name. It was difficult to tell his age because his head was shaved, but he looked around forty-five. His body looked younger, lean and muscled from walking the countryside so many years. His feet were as thickly padded on the bottom as shoe soles.

Rita went in to get tea and offered it around in cups. Swamiji took his politely, but in a minute he got up and washed his coconut shell. He then poured the tea into it and drank with loud, appreciative slurps. A wandering *sadhu*, a holy man, has no attachments, but I imagine he does get fond of his coconut shell. When a kind host gives him food, the shell becomes a bowl. When he drinks from a river, it becomes a cup. And when it rains, it becomes a hat. To have a *sadhu* ask for shelter or food at your house is considered a great blessing. This particular man had stopped this way to see Vinod's family ever since his father was a boy, I was told. So it was a delightful surprise to find him on their doorstep just when Vinod had come from America after so many years.

Swamiji was very lively and extraordinarily interested to hear about America.

"Did you all really come from Pathal?" he would ask and laugh. Pathal is the word for the underworld. Dusty and still smelling of incense, we stayed on the veranda to answer his bubbling questions. Weren't they primitive people in America? Did they really eat meat and kill each other all the time? How did they fly through the air? Swamiji had walked everywhere, from Sri Lanka to the Himalayas, but he knew little about the world. His opinions were utterly naive, and you could not help but be smitten by his innocence. As I sat trying to explain to him what a heart attack was, I thought that I had never met anyone so unmistakably joyful.

Swamiji didn't let us go to bed for hours. His entire existence was one long search for God and enlightenment. He would talk to anyone, at any length, who was interested in the truth. The Tibetans, he said, had had valuable things to tell him. He had walked there in the snow a few winters earlier. He went barefoot, wrapped in his one cloth, depending on strangers for food. Sometimes no one gave him anything to eat for four or five days, but he didn't care. He walked for a long time and finally found some Tibetan lamas in a cave, very remote and inaccessible. They had intriguing views to impart to a seeker, but their ways were strange. Swamiji had never seen priests who ate meat. It must be the cold that makes it necessary, he thought. He had to decline their offer of food until one of them caught on and boiled some wheat grain for him. As he walked back over the Himalayas, he found it curious that men were shooting in his direction and setting off explosions all around him. We told Swamiji that India and China had been waging war on the border that year. Oh.

Swamiji had just visited a locally famous saint, who was known as Mast Ram. The name means "mad for God." He had not stopped meditating for at least fifty years. He rarely moved, and the only way he could be fed was by having his disciples pry open his mouth to squirt in some fruit juice once in a while. People who went to see him argued over the fixed expression he wore on his face. Some said it was an expression of perfect bliss. Others said it looked merely idiotic. But everyone liked visiting this saint once in a while, like the Taj Mahal. We asked Swamiji what he thought of the saint. Oh, he said, he's as *mast* as ever, and he laughed delightedly.

We all slept late the next morning. Around ten o'clock we paid our respects to Vinod's ninety-year-old grandfather. He was very alert and lively. His secluded life pleased him. He told us that Swamiji had been up at four in the morning, the usual time for his devotions. He got breakfast for himself by climbing one of the mango trees and drinking out of a stream.

We told the old man that we were now on our way to Rishikesh. He looked very happy at this news. Rishikesh lies at the foothills of the Himalayas, very near the source of the Ganges, and is a traditional place for ashrams and holy men. Beyond it lies an area almost untouched by the world for as long as anyone knows: Uttar Kashi, the valley of the saints. We were making our trip on a whim, really, because we wanted to see Maharishi Mahesh Yogi, the founder of Transcendental Meditation. When Swamiji heard this the night before, he had been very pleased. He had once seen Maharishi, many years earlier, and considered him a great sage. This was when Maharishi lived as a young man in Uttar Kashi, before he came out into the West. What we didn't allude to in front of the *sadhu* or Vinod's grandfather was that our trip had come up because we felt attracted to Maharishi's teaching.

The time came to leave. We found Swamiji in the yard and said farewell. He kept talking and holding us back, but we finally got into the Ambassador. The driver rumbled off, lurching over the rocks in the road. For a long time, through the back window we could see Swamiji waving joyfully to us. Then he couldn't contain himself. He ran up to the car and paced beside it, covered in clouds of dust. I was startled and a little worried for him. We must have been going at least ten miles an hour, but the *sadhu* kept up with us, his beaming face constantly at my window. Finally he had to stop, after we turned onto the main road, and I asked Vinod exactly how old Swamiji was.

"I don't know," Vinod said. "He's always looked about the same as he does now, ever since I was a kid."

Then I asked Vinod's father the same question.

"I don't know, either," he said. "He looked about the same when I was young, too."

"Could you guess his age even roughly?" I asked.

Vinod's father added numbers in his head. "I suppose he

has to be about seventy," he said. I was more than impressed.

The conventions of spirituality are still followed in India, though people have changed to conform to the modern world. A man like Vinod's father can run his textile business, traveling with his reckless chauffeur in a sixteen-hour day from one end of India to the other. Then he will return home and sit on the floor with the family guru to unwind. It is a nice way to unwind, hearing about *Vedanta*, the joys of unity, and the uselessness of worldly attachment. Even if he discusses renunciation with a glass of twelve-year-old Scotch in his hand, Vinod's father seems perfectly content with his two worlds.

Vinod felt equally content. He was a generation younger and more mobile. He had moved to America in the seventies to attend Harvard and M.I.T., and eventually he set up his own computer business. That is how I got to know him. He did not have the family guru with him, but at least in me he had someone who would talk about enlightenment anytime he wanted. We did it the right way, sitting on the floor and often drinking Scotch. Every morning and evening, Vinod performed *puja*. His father would be doing the same thing at his rural home in the Kulu mountains, as all their ancestors had done.

For a long time after we met, Vinod was the only one who practiced meditation, some form of concentration his guru had taught him, while I simply sat and talked. Then, after three years, he took up a practice with me that we called *real* meditation. It wasn't anything the family guru taught or even understood. You did not need to purify yourself or light a candle or even pray to follow the practice. It was not renunciation at all. Our guiding idea was something quite new, the integration of mind and body to the ultimate degree. And it took place in the here and now, long before *sanyasa*. A devout father could only be suspicious.

I had discovered Transcendental Meditation on my own in 1980. Quite by chance, browsing through a secondhand bookstore in Boston, I ran across a TM book on the dollar shelf. It looked interesting, and I took it home with me. What I knew about systems of meditation was practically nothing, but I had assumptions about them. It is impossible to come from India and not have a set of strong impressions about meditation. To me, meditation meant controlling the mind. The saying we all heard growing up was that the mind is like a drunken monkey, leaping this way and that in its maddened desires. Or it is like a flame that wavers in the wind and cannot be still. Or it is a wild elephant that can only be tamed by tying it to a post and waiting until exhaustion wore out the wildness.

Meditation was the post. It was meant for hermits and the religiously inclined. It led to inner peace, but primarily for those who renounced the world. If you were advanced enough and willing to give up everything else in life, then meditation held out a precious reward. It broke the bonds of ignorance. I didn't disagree with any of this exactly, but it could wait.

My main reason for picking up the TM book was that I sensed its novelty. Nothing quite like it was taught at home. I later heard Maharishi Mahesh Yogi make a remark about teaching: knowledge is like water; to be pure, it must keep running. The stream of wisdom that flows through India is very broad and very long, but no one would say that it is fresh. If a wandering monk decides to sit down in the middle of the street to go into meditation, then the cars will simply have to drive around him. The cows stepped around him three thousand years ago. Why should anything change? Modern people in India may regret, and regret very deeply, that the tradition of enlightenment no longer appeals to us. But we also sense that the knowledge is stagnant and therefore not pure.

We Indians still believe that our ancient texts contain a legacy for all people. The promise of Ayurveda, for instance, is that it is a medicine for mankind. Yet every phrase in the *Rig Veda* or *Bhagavad-Gita* seems to have given rise to a different sect. And each one wants to compete for the truth. Every village has a priest, guru, or vaidya who acts as the resident authority. In the clamor of their chants and prayers, their beliefs and dogmas, one never steps into the clear stream of knowledge. At best, one steps into a different temple. And all temples in India are very old.

The book on Transcendental Meditation managed to finesse my prejudices, at least the worst ones, by not confronting the old ways at all. The language actually seemed to apply equally to everyone. Instead of ignorance and bondage, it talked of stress accumulating in the body. In place of liberation, it talked of getting to the point where the stress has been dissolved. Drunken monkeys and chained elephants were not referred to because mind control or concentration was not allowed. The whole business of working strenuously for enlightenment had been dropped. Correct meditation was an effortless process that led to deeper relaxation. It released stress. Spiritual attainment was still the great goal it had been for uncounted centuries, but it was meaningless to dwell on it as long as the body and mind were unprepared. I found this sensible enough. The process of stress release also sounded believable. And I could use it, since I was not a stranger to stress.

At that time I was very proud of my beeper. Doctors wear beepers on their hips the way marshals used to wear six-guns. When you have a beeper, you don't forget that you are a doctor. Anyone can call you, day or night. You don't have to miss any emergencies. You boost your nerves to a state of constant vigilance, monitoring all your cases all the time. My beeper was especially vigilant. It beeped for me in restaurants. It beeped in the car, at concerts, and in bed. I found out about pancreatic tumors while I was eating veal Florentine. When I got up to answer a call, people looked at me with a little irritation and a lot of respect — a doctor was going to save a patient's life.

But my days were blurring into nights. I was drinking black coffee by the hour and smoking at least a pack of cigarettes a day. I had acquired a taste for whiskey in the evening. My schedule kept my stomach mildly churning all the time, and I never stopped carrying the burning taste of gastric juice in my mouth. The idea of stress management was in the air. TM had abundant research to prove that it relieved stress. So why not?

I found that the technique was easy, as advertised. It also made very little claim upon my time, since the sittings for meditation were only fifteen to twenty minutes long, twice a day — nothing at all compared to what is required of a devotee in India. Nor did you have to possess a devotee's strong beliefs. My TM teacher emphasized that one could sit with eyes closed thinking, I don't believe in this, I don't believe in this, and the technique would still work. I was told, however, not to force thoughts of any kind, for or against. The key to the practice was innocence. The ideal attitude, my teacher said, was to meditate for one's twenty minutes, get up from the chair, and forget that the meditation had ever taken place.

I am going into a few of these particulars because the meditation did work, beautifully. Within a week I stopped drinking, the last habit I had picked up under the pressure of my work. Two weeks later I quit smoking. This had been a more serious problem, yet one morning on rounds I noticed that three days had gone by without a cigarette. It came to me like that, as an afterthought. I told myself that I must have lost the taste, as in fact I had, but the actual change happened in my mind: I didn't *need* the taste. After a few slips backward, the need never returned.

These few improvements in my life made a dramatic difference out of proportion to the way they sound on paper. I began once again to feel extraordinarily well. My spirits rose noticeably day by day until I was feeling too buoyant to talk to anyone about it without embarrassing myself. I only told my friend Vinod indirectly. Wishing not to offend him, I returned to his house at midnight after one of our discussions and left my paperback about TM on his doorstep. I felt foolish in the morning, but within three hours he called me and asked when he could start.

Now there were two of us following the practice. We were calling it "real" meditation because we felt that an undeniable breakthrough had been made in a tradition that cashes in more on legends than results. TM asks, fairly enough, to be judged by results, by improvements in daily life. In TM they seem well aware that modern Western people, having no reason to respect meditation historically, will accept claims for it only if they are scientifically credible.

That means experimentation. TM has obliged its skeptics, as far as that can be done, by conducting literally hundreds of experiments. The first ones concentrated on how the physiology responds to meditation, because the best angle to take in the West is that meditation brings relaxation. (An anecdote everyone in TM knows concerns the first story ever printed about Maharishi in this country. It appeared in a San Francisco newspaper in 1958: "Yogi Teaches New Sleeping Method." When he saw it, Maharishi's heart sank. "I came to wake up the West," he commented, "and they wanted to learn how to sleep.") TM research later moved into a dozen other fields. If the technique can promote creativity, improve health, raise grades in school, or help you run a maze faster, then the TM researchers have found out about it.

This all sounds like self-improvement. Vinod and I were happy enough to improve, although we did not feel that deficient to begin with. We were essentially healthy and confident in ourselves. We had built careers and marriages. We felt adequately intelligent, adequately able to work and to love. Something deeper needed to be stirred. We had talked about the source of fulfillment that Indian wisdom located in the self. We fully expected, after thousands of revolutions of the wheel of karma, to reach it. Now an astonishing thing was happening. The self was appearing to us, not at the end of our progress, but at the beginning.

In this meditation, the first experience was remarkable. As the teacher had suggested, it was quiet and serene and without strain. You didn't seem to be doing anything. But something more personal was occurring, like a curtain being drawn aside at midnight. Suddenly you see what needs to be seen. One of the Upanishads says, "When the mind is overcome by its own radiance, then dreams are no longer seen: joy and peace come to the body." I was waking up to that, lightly and peacefully. But the new life was so new that for the first months I hardly dared to look into it.

Vinod and I grew shy about putting it into words, for all that we had talked about it before. Wisdom and perfection had been words for us, slippery words that all at once had turned into — what? Something very desirable yet unbelievable. I remember being so taken with bewildered happiness that I said, "It's true." Just that. Vinod understood. The inner genius had to move slowly for fear that its joy would be too much. The heart had had to be protected for so long while it was small. We did not fool ourselves. Perfection had not seized us all at once. We couldn't even have said very coherently what perfection meant. It was early. Our noses had just caught the smell of sea breezes. But we knew we would reach the sea.

It is a miserable ride to Rishikesh once the paved road ends and the unpaved ones, the *kutcha* roads, begin. The chauffeur dodged around the cows and honked right up the backs of the camel drivers. Rita and I were not so frightened now, more because we had tougher nerves than because it was any safer. The outskirts of Rishikesh, once we arrived, looked disappointingly like those of any commercial town. We left the car and started walking toward the Ganges. Here the river is much closer to its source than at Haridwar. All the ashrams are on the other side of the river. The holy men call the land on our side "the mud." Any part of the world beyond their valley is just that, the mud.

To cross the river, we had to negotiate a narrow footbridge. We were apprehensive, not because of the rushing, mountain-fed torrent below, but because of the weird assembly that gathers every day on the bridge. You thread your way as best you can past bodies contorted into bizarre postures, tattooed *sadhus* and half-crazy beggars. Some are deformed or intentionally disfigured, presumably out of religious passion. Rita refused to look. Vinod and I took her hands to guide her, but we weren't looking too closely ourselves. On the other side, we reached a rugged pathway leading past all the ashrams. Once we had walked half an hour, through evergreen forest and beside the rushing white-capped water, the sight of those beings faded, like a dream of purgatory.

Maharishi's site on the Ganges is not an ashram, in the sense that disciples come to be with their guru. Transcendental Meditation had dropped that, too, which accounts for its self-sufficiency outside the narrow confines of the Indian tradition. But by the same token, TM needed many teachers, and to train them Maharishi used Rishikesh for his Indian academy. When we got to the gate, we saw a group of simple brick buildings and an enclave of one-room dwellings. These were the modern replacements for Himalayan caves. We also found out from the gatekeeper that Maharishi wasn't there. Why hadn't we inquired ahead? We felt silly.

But he put us in the hands of the director of the Rishikesh academy. He was a Sanskrit teacher who had given up his studies to work for TM. As we chatted in his small room, I noticed that he seemed at home with us from the first minute. He had lively eyes, good large Indian eyes. He talked like a man who was always happy. When Vinod's father asked him whether he planned on eventually returning to university life and his family, the young man pointed outside.

"There is the mountain, so I have my father. There is the river, so I have my mother," he said. Then he pointed to Maharishi's picture on the mantel. "And there is my teacher. Why would I want to leave?" He said all this with such simplicity that we all grew reflective. His eyes looked at us with a glow — the fire of aspiration, I thought. He wanted perfection. No one can judge another's enlightenment, but I felt sure that this stranger would not lower his eyes before anybody's. His gaze had love in it; therefore it had tremendous power.

I thought about the difference between happiness in India and happiness in the West. In India it can be a more daring venture, risking ordinary pleasures for something supreme. It seems quite natural in India that a person might want nothing else than to reach the goal of existence and to live in bliss. I considered this man's joyous face and the clear outline of his life. It was not possible just then to want anything less for myself.

But the fuzzy outlines of my own life scratched me. I found his joyfulness too much. I felt a little demonic urge to prick it.

"What about those people on the bridge?" I asked him. I was sorry the moment I opened my mouth. I was being unfair. All at once he looked quite grave.

"They are why we are here," he said. An expression of sadness came into his face for a moment. The contrast between Maharishi's teaching and what we saw on the bridge stood out vividly in my mind. Then our host asked us if we wished to meet with Satyanand, a contemporary of Maharishi's and completely devoted to him, who had, like him, taken holy orders as a monk. We said yes immediately, grateful for the honor. He led us to the hut Satyanand occupied.

We found him alone, sitting quietly on a divan in lotus position. His room was dim, and it took a few seconds for our eyes to adjust. Sitting with him in the half shadow, one felt Satyanand's great serenity. This is a marvel with Indian sages, that they lend everyone near them a portion of their inner silence. He greeted us with a smile. He wore his hair and beard untrimmed, as monks do; both were nearly white. His dress was a monk's dhoti, a simple garment wound from one piece of white silk.

"Do you meditate?" he asked after a while. He used the familiar word *dhyan*, but he meant TM. We told him that we had learned in Boston. He laughed. "Indians go to Boston to learn *dhyan* — it's wonderful!" And he laughed again, not at us, but with a lovely innocence. Then Satyanand began to talk animatedly. He told us that his thoughts had flashed to the possibility that everyone would find a place, near or far, to learn *dhyan*. Maharishi had dedicated his life to that goal, and his success had surpassed anything India had produced in many generations.

We stayed on this topic as an hour passed, but I remember also that Satyanand told us a story, a very touching one. It concerns Ravana, the villain of the *Ramayana*. The story comes at the end of the adventures that ensue after Ravana has stolen Sita, using the stratagem of the deer to lure Rama away from his bride.

As a villain, Ravana is supremely exciting. By abducting Sita, he sets a deadly combat in motion. As king of the demons, possessing tremendous powers over fire, wind, and storms, he is the only fit challenger to the divine Rama. Like most boys, I thought him wonderful, the best character in my grandmother's stories. Ravana could hurl mountains and was gifted with the most ferocious and formidable of evil geniuses. But Satyanand brought him up as if he were good.

"Oh, don't you know about Ravana as he really was?" he asked. Then he proceeded to recount an episode from the *Ramayana* that he must have had his own sources for, since I have never again found it told in the following way.

Ravana has all the extraordinary powers called *sidhis*. He also knows all the scriptures better than anyone alive. His advantage is that he has ten heads. Each stands for a different Veda or Upanishad. At the outset of his story he lacks for nothing — power, wealth, lands, magic abilities. He is a master of pulse diagnosis and all the arts of medicine as well. But he is not enlightened. This preys upon Ravana's mind until he can think of nothing else. He is convinced that immediate enlightenment is all that he wants, but he does not know how to go about getting it.

He decides to ask for advice. After a long journey into the Himalayas, he finds a very wise and venerable rishi, a sage above sages, and asks him the way to enlightenment. The sage advises Ravana to enjoy what he has; in time, enlightenment will come. But Ravana is not satisfied. I will sacrifice everything I have, he declares, to obtain liberation in this lifetime. Wait, the rishi cautions him again. Ravana refuses. He demands to know what it will take to become enlightened. Now.

The rishi is not afraid of Ravana. He ponders the matter and then answers that Ravana can only become enlightened in this lifetime if he dies, and in a special way. He must be killed by an arrow through the heart shot from the bow of God himself. Ravana decides to go home and think about it. He sits and thinks, but soon the burning desire to become enlightened possesses him again. He will do it.

How can he provoke God to kill him, though? God is compassionate. Ravana hits upon the perfect plan. He will abduct God's wife. He goes in search of Sita, the devoted wife of Prince Rama. This sounds peculiar to a Western ear, but in the *Ramayana* the hero is more than a prince and a warrior. Rama embodies every perfection of the human spirit — courage, intelligence, fidelity, compassion, love — but he is also an incarnation of God. The story does not distinguish between his two aspects: they are simply Rama. So it is perfectly possible for God to lose his kingdom, as Prince Rama does, and to go wandering penniless with his bride.

Ravana succeeds in stealing Sita and taking her to his kingdom in Ceylon. Rama pursues them, but he is stopped by the open sea that separates Ceylon from the mainland. He has no boat and nothing with which to rent a boat, so he invokes the aid of Hanuman, king of the monkeys, who orders his subjects to build a magical monkey bridge across the sea. Rama crosses with his forces. He encamps before the castle of his enemy, and the battle is ready to be joined.

But one thing is still needed, a *yagya*. This is a sacred rite of propitiation, and no battle can begin without it. To perform a *yagya*, however, one needs a brahmin priest. Although he is God, Rama is not a brahmin. By birth he comes from the caste of warriors and kings. Nor is anyone else in his army a brahmin, since they are monkeys. Then someone remembers that Ravana himself, who knows all the Vedas, must be a brahmin. An invitation is sent, asking him to come down and kindly perform the *yagya*.

Ravana appears before Rama and agrees to act as priest for the rite, but there is the matter of the ceremonial gift that is expected as payment in return. He turns to Rama with disdain. "What can you possibly give me?" he says. "You may be a prince, but you have no kingdom anymore. You don't have money or possessions, and I have your wife. What can you give me to perform your *yagya*?"

Rama considers this for a moment. Then he asks Ravana, "What do you want? Ask me."

At this, Ravana sees his chance at last. He prostrates himself before God and says, "I have only one wish in the world,

Lord. However the battle may end tomorrow, if I have to die on the field, let it be from one of your arrows, yours alone, and may you shoot me through the heart." Greatly moved, Lord Rama agrees.

Satyanand ended his story quite late. The Himalayan twilight was growing deep around us. The silence in the room was immensely deeper. All of us took our leave, and the group proceeded back toward the bridge, walking quickly and without much talk. We wanted to make it back to Rishikesh before nightfall. We succeeded, but as soon as we started the car, it began to rain. The *kutcha* roads seemed slower and rockier than ever. Our ride home was going to be very long, I thought. Delhi might as well have been on another continent.

The rain gushed across the windshield. Lightning flashed so close that we became alarmed — this had to be one of the worst storms of the year. We crept on through the dark, feeling a little tired of one another. Then the moment came that I hate. Two glaring headlights bore down upon us and drew closer. It was a bus, and we would have to find a way for it and us to get by each other. Our driver waited until the last minute, as usual, and then he swerved. The bus made it by without touching us. Suddenly we crashed.

The impact shattered our headlights, and we found ourselves in pitch darkness. But we soon discovered what we had hit. It was a bullock cart, the last one in a line twenty carts long. A night caravan was carrying goods to the next town. We got out to inspect the damage. It was much worse to our car than to what we had hit. The driver of the cart had been asleep, and the crash did nothing worse than startle him. He and the other drivers gathered around, concerned that we were all right.

Once everyone saw that everyone else was unhurt, the drivers let us pass, smiling and waving. We had one small piece of luck at least. Having to stay behind a bullock caravan is almost as bad as hitting one. The main road appeared in an hour. I sat thinking about the arrow to Ravana's heart and the young stranger who knew that he wanted perfection. They both understood the fire of aspiration. No one said much. Our families in Delhi would be worried, and now they weren't likely to see us before two in the morning.

Then Vinod's father began to sing, "Mano, budhi, ahankar." It was a favorite of his, one of the same *bhajans* that we had heard the women singing in Haridwar. The words mean, "I am not mind, I am not intellect, I am not ego." The song has a beautiful melody, and we all knew it. Vinod joined in first, and then some barrier broke and the rest of us, including the driver, followed.

"I have no death, I have no fear," we sang. "I see no caste in anyone. I have no father and no mother, I was not even born. I have no friends and no relations. I have no master and no disciple. I am only blissful consciousness. I am God. I am God."

The driver was in especially fine voice. He must have been very happy to be pardoned so easily.

10

Return of the Rishi

IN 1975, four years after our daughter, Mallika, was born, Rita became pregnant again. We hoped this baby would be a boy. If so, Rita had picked out for him the name Kabir. The word *kabir* means "great" in Arabic, but it is also the name of a poet beloved by all Indians. A baby named Kabir, instead of something Hindu, would certainly sound Moslem to Indian ears, but we did not care. Every group — Hindu, Moslem, even Sikh and Christian — has put forward proofs that Kabir is theirs. It seemed enough just to love him. I would come home to find Rita practicing the sound "Kabir Chopra, Kabir Chopra," making sure that the name was right. By the time our baby was due, she had her heart set on it.

Neither of us had actually read Kabir, but we had heard his songs since childhood. They were sung in our homes at the gatherings called *kirtan,* which generally precedes afternoon tea. My mother's still comes on the first Tuesday of each month, and everyone, not just family and friends, shows up. It is a mysterious thing, in fact, how people find a *kirtan.* Somehow it is just in the air. All sorts of locals arrive without notice at the front door. The musicians set up their instruments, usually a small set of drums, or *tabla,* and a foot-pedal harmonium to carry the tune. Everyone else seats himself on the carpet.

The guests come in high spirits, not what you might expect at sacred singing. Indians know how to enjoy holidays, and for the audience a *kirtan* is like a holiday in the middle of the afternoon. The women sit on one side of the room, the men on the other, but Hindus, Moslems, and Christians freely mix. There are special *kirtan* singers who also show up for the occasion. As the singing goes on, however, everyone gets carried along into singing sooner or later.

The songs are very familiar and very old. They manage to be popular and devotional at the same time, which may account for why they have lasted. A generous portion were composed by Kabir five centuries ago. His are among the happiest, but they are also the ones filled with mystery:

> There is a land where doubt and sorrows do not reign,
> where the terror of death is unknown.
> Its woods are floored with the flowers of spring, and a
> fragrance, "I am He," floats on the wind.
> There, the bee of the heart is drowning in
> nectar and desires no other joy.

A *kirtan* has festivity in it; Kabir gives it wonder. You can anticipate his songs because they generally follow a familiar pattern. A dull, orthodox fellow called the *sadhu* has come to challenge Kabir, a simple weaver, about the secrets of existence. The *sadhu* knows the Scriptures inside out, but he has no idea that Kabir is a saint. Soon he learns, as the words of Kabir well up from his rapturous heart. This common weaver knows human life to its depths. What he knows, he has discovered in himself, and he has no patience for orthodoxy:

> There is only water in the holy pools,
> I know, because I went swimming in them.

All the idols carved out of wood are silent,
I know, because I called out to them.
The sacred books are nothing but words,
I saw through them just this morning.

Then, to make sure that his point comes home to the *sadhu*, there is a tag at the end of many songs that begins, "Kabir says." Sometimes the tag conveys a pungent rebuke: "Kabir says, what you haven't lived through, you do not know to be true."

More often, however, the ending is inspiring. There is one song about a woman who sits at her spinning wheel extolling her husband, who has gone away. Here is the ending: "Kabir says, I am that woman, I am weaving the cloth of night and day. When my Lover comes and I touch his feet, I shall give him the gift of my tears."

Kabir is embraced by the common people because he speaks this intimately. He is a master of hushed adoration, but he has a lion's confidence, too. He is that rarity, a knower of reality, which all the Upanishads glorify. We sing Kabir's songs out of longing, ultimately. He is what we want to be — utterly free of sorrow and fear. From wherever his spirit is, Kabir speaks as soul to soul: "You have slept for millions on millions of years, won't you this morning wake up?" When I hear this at *kirtan*, I wish I could wake up to be in the land of Kabir. No one else has made the inner and outer worlds so closely one. He sings continually of the one life, the one joy, and the one creation. He devotes himself to wisdom, compassion, kindness, and understanding, but in reality he has devoted himself to only one thing, his ecstatic love:

"Kabir says, I have lifted the curtain and looked beneath. Whoever has loved will understand."

Kabir lived to a great age, some say to a hundred and twenty. After he died, legend says that two factions laid claim to the body. The Moslems wanted to take it for entombment;

the Hindus wanted to take it to be burned. The dispute grew bitter, and just when there seemed to be no way to resolve it, Kabir himself appeared in a vision. He instructed his followers to go together and lift the shroud that covered his remains. They went, and in place of a body they found heaps of fresh flowers. Amazed by this miracle, his followers were reconciled on the spot. The flowers were divided, half going to the Moslems, who placed them reverently in a marble tomb, half to the Hindus, who burned them and cast their ashes over the sacred Ganges.

As it happened, Rita did give birth to a boy, but he wasn't named Kabir. Having a Moslem name would have caused too many ripples in my family, and besides, they said, everyone knows that Kabir was a foundling. At least give your son a name that shows he has a respectable father. We decided to bend with the wind. I might never have given the weaver of night and day another thought except at *kirtan*. He comes to mind now, however, because since then I have met his likeness.

It was in 1985, two years after our trip to Rishikesh, that I got an opportunity to meet Maharishi. When my chance came, I grew unexpectedly shy. A young psychologist at Harvard was doing a study to show the benefits of Transcendental Meditation for older people. He had some quite good results and I was very interested, so we talked every once in a while. One day he announced that Maharishi had come for a visit to America, which he had not done for several years. Would I like to go to Washington, D.C., and be introduced?

Whatever else we are, doctors are not good followers. I made excuses for a day or two. My psychologist friend continued to call me, and I could tell that he wondered at my reluctance. But I had placed a long distance between myself and any idea of having a guru. I would not have started TM in the first place if it hadn't allowed me to meditate on my own. In that respect, even though I was raised in India, I am a child of my times. There is a saying in India: "Four things in life you must cherish: first the guru, then your parents, next your wife and children, and finally the nation." No one knows how old the saying is, old enough to seem permanent. But the changeless has changed. I talked to Rita about the troublesome invitation, and we decided that our curiosity was stronger than our timidity. We went.

If I was worried about my integrity in public, I needn't have. We found ourselves at the back of a dark auditorium peering over five hundred heads and around four massive pillars. The workmen had barely finished putting in a new ceiling. Plaster dust kept falling on my lapels. The air system was rumbling in the walls behind my back, but I didn't feel any air. I managed just barely to discern that the remote figure on the stage was indeed Maharishi, dressed in white silk and seated in lotus position on a divan. He rarely stirred, and even from a distance, one got the impression of immaculate stillness. As he talked, he gestured with a flower in his hand. His voice was unusually varied, rising and falling, often breaking out in a laugh. Not every speaker that evening was equally brilliant, and once or twice you heard a thunk as Maharishi's flower tilted forward and hit the microphone.

He spent several hours discussing the revival of Ayurveda with various doctors and Indian pundits. It sounded interesting, but we had been plunked in the last row of a musty room. We had a plane to catch, and the next two hours were apparently going to be more of the same. As discreetly as we could, Rita and I walked out.

We felt something between relief and disappointment. On the way out, we stopped for a glass of water, then began to make our way through the empty lobby. At just that moment, the doors to the hall opened and out came Maharishi. He walked very fast for such a small man. A group of people trailed behind him, but without warning he veered away from where they were going, toward the elevators, and walked to his left instead, right up to Rita and me.

In his arms he carried a loose bundle of flowers, which had been given to him in the hall. He picked out a long-stemmed red rose and handed it to Rita, then another and handed it to me.

"Can you come up?" he asked us.

Feeling a little dazed, I looked over at Rita. We were both thinking about our flight home half an hour later. I didn't know what to say, and I noticed that my heart had started to pound violently in my chest.

"We have a plane to catch, Maharishi," I said. He laughed.

"Oh, can't you come up?" he repeated. We decided to go.

Upstairs we found ourselves in a conference room decorated from floor to ceiling in pink. We sat on overstuffed pink chairs; Maharishi sat in lotus position on a white divan, the only nonpink furniture in the room. Rita and I had seen his picture many times, so he seemed familiar to us already, except that his untrimmed monk's beard now had a wider ribbon of white in the middle. I am short next to Americans, but he is almost tiny. His shoulders and forearms look very strong, but underneath his white silk dhoti, one notices the slender frame. I remember our conversation well, but more striking to me at the time was my reaction to him. Maharishi Mahesh Yogi is a name that suggests a story. Like *kabir*, *maharishi* is a word. It combines *maha* or "great" and *rishi* or "sage." The part of the name that we would call a given name is Mahesh. And *yogi* means "in union." A man named Mahesh has attained union and become a great sage.

His manner was quite simple, but at the same time, as he chatted with us, one could not imagine paying attention to anyone else. At a point very early in our meeting, I noticed that my own attention, exposed to his, had become very concentrated. And without any effort, my mind had fallen silent. No thoughts moved through it, and there wasn't the usual ricochet of stray impressions — just silence. This seemed an extraordinarily pleasant state to be in, because I felt completely unself-conscious. It didn't usually cross my mind that I carried the weight of my own self-consciousness until that moment, when it dropped off. I felt no desire to look important or to impress Maharishi. There are seekers in India who wander naked all their lives. They have renounced everything, including clothes. They call themselves the sky-clad. For that hour, I could have sat sky-clad and not been embarrassed.

Maharishi asked us about ourselves. We started to tell him. I mentioned that I was a doctor, that I had practiced TM for four years, that I had written a book.

"You must be very smart if you can write books," Maharishi said.

I didn't know what to reply to that — Maharishi had himself written two inspired books — so I forged ahead. I got to the point of saying that I was an assistant professor of medicine. His face lit up.

"Oh, then you must be *really* smart," he said, and he laughed delightedly. There wasn't a hint that he was poking fun. "And what is your specialty?" he asked.

I told him it was endocrinology.

"That's excellent," Maharishi said. "It connects everything in the body, doesn't it? Like a net." He made a gesture with his hands. I was surprised he knew that, but he was exactly right.

"Do you know much about Ayurveda?" he asked me. I shook my head. "You should learn," he said, "because it is such a simple way of approaching medicine. Everything around us is change, but it all takes place against a background that is unchanging. Against everything in the relative world is a background of the absolute. Ayurveda says (here he might have quoted a verse in Sanskrit) that behind mortality is the aspect of immortality. The goal of Ayurveda is to restore this multiplicity to that absolute, to unity."

Consciousness is our link back to the unchanging, he explained, because our consciousness rises from the absolute in the same way that plants, rocks, and all physical things arise. The raw material for everything in the universe is consciousness.

"Nature thinks the way we do," I remember Maharishi saying. And that was the key. If Nature is thinking everything in the same way, then it has thought of all remedies. For it, physical existence is just one theme working its way through a billion variations. The secret was not to be so distracted by the variations that you missed the theme.

"You see?" Maharishi said. "Everything is orderly because everything is intelligence. Food is intelligence, the plants are intelligence. What we take in as nourishment we convert to our own intelligence. We don't have to know anything else once we know how to bring intelligence back into line. Sickness is interrupted intelligence, but we can bring it back into line. That's all we do from our side. Then Nature takes care of it."

Maharishi did not lay out the details of Ayurveda for us that night, but he made the theme vividly clear. Health and disease are connected like variations on one melody. But disease is a wrong variation, a distortion of the theme.

Ayurveda's approach to physical disorders is not basically physical at all. Faced with any illness, the vaidya turns directly to Nature's intelligence, where he finds the real cure. The herbs, minerals, and metals that he uses "think the way we do." For every part of our bodies, Nature provides a substance to complement it. Medicine then consists of letting like speak to like. Take the remedy whole, as Nature provides it, and through its similarity to ourselves, it can restore health. Ayurveda worked because it corrects a distortion in consciousness — a wrong wiggle goes back into line.

Maharishi talked in this vein for two hours. It was a remarkable experience listening to him. He was stitching together, very simply and deftly, a new world. It arose from awareness. Everything that happened in it — the creation of stars and galaxies, the grass growing, the flow of the tides, eating a meal — came down to the same thing, an unending transformation of the one intelligence.

At around eleven our meeting came to an end.

"You must come and look at Ayurveda with us," Maharishi told me as I got up. "Will you? It will make your job much easier." He laughed, and as a parting gesture he very carefully picked out two more roses. He must have scrutinized a dozen before he found the right ones. He asked us to give them to our children. We took one last glimpse of him in the pink room, and the next minute we were alone in the elevator. As happy as Rita and I felt, our thoughts still turned to the plane that had taken off two hours earlier. It was the last one back to Boston.

On an impulse, we went to the airport anyway. There were no later flights, we were told, but by chance, all the earlier flights had been delayed on the eastern corridor, and our plane was still on the ground. The ticket agent said it was one of the longest delays of the year — we were very lucky. As we headed home, I thought about Ayurveda and Maharishi's desire for me to become involved in it. Now that I was away from him, my inner silence evaporated, and the buzzing of thoughts started up again.

The difference between silence and even the faintest thought is immense. For anyone who has not experienced it, the flavor of inner silence is unknown. Those who have experienced it find it irresistible. I have heard Maharishi say that complete silence is the nature of pure awareness. A mind in that state is like a lake, vast and completely still, crystal clear to the bottom, but so delicate that it registers the fall of a single petal on its surface. Compared to the din and confusion of our thoughts, the thoughts that pass through silence are like the shadows of clouds passing across the water's surface.

Some silence remained in my awareness, but now it was spoiled by anxiety. Over and over, a thought repeated itself to me: "Don't become an outsider." I was being asked to look outside science. I didn't see how I could. Perhaps Ayurveda would be the science of tomorrow, but what was it today? I thought about my standing as a doctor. Ayurveda is not licensed medicine in America. I wasn't being asked to practice Ayurveda, simply to look into it. But part of me said that I had a lot to lose. Another part, at home in silence, didn't have an opinion. It saw no problems at all — but that part was very new.

I lay in bed thinking about Maharishi himself. The tradition of wisdom in India has been passed down from one person to another, from teacher to disciple, as far back as one can go. This may seem a more fragile way than written records, but in reality it has been much more durable. The teacher, or *acharya*, embodies the truth he talks about. If he can effectively teach it, his disciple becomes the next embodiment, and in that way, generation after generation, the living links are forged. The truth may sink from public sight, but somewhere it is flowing through a sage. A mind that is truly enlightened does not think the truth, it creates it. That is why a true *acharya* is very rare.

The strength of the *acharya* tradition lies in its sameness, repeating itself like a series of dawns from epoch to epoch. However different one teacher may be from another, they are still alike, and they are all linked together. Through them, wisdom renews itself in every generation.

Well-versed teachers in India all know the Veda, but they do not necessarily turn it into living truth. The only way to know whether a teacher can create truth is by one's own awareness. Wisdom is judged by what it can do, not by how it sounds. It should alter life and make it strong. I had no doubt, after practicing his meditation, that Maharishi was anything less than his name implied. He is a great sage, a knower and teacher of reality. It had been unnecessary for me to seek him out as a guru, because, by a stroke of genius, Maharishi has compressed the *acharya* and placed him inside every meditator. If we want to look for the one who will enlighten us, we do not have to go beyond our own doorstep.

I thought about this and about the trust Maharishi seemed so willing to place in me, an utter stranger. As he talked to us, his look had been unforgettably tender and humane. In one of Kabir's best songs comes the line, "Kabir says, forget about your illusions and stand fast in what you are." The first thing I told Rita the next morning was that I had decided to go back to Washington.

More than anything he said, I had been affected by the deep silence that Maharishi emanates. It has a remarkable power; to cultivate such silence in ourselves is to have the power, too. Maharishi calls it the power that governs the universe because it is pure intelligence, unchanging and completely self-contained. When people experience it within themselves on a wide scale, and allow it gently to remove the frustrations of life, then the world will be fundamentally altered. Behind all our changing thoughts and emotions, we have yet to investigate the background, which is the unchanging. It is silent, and the sages tell us that it is love: "Kabir says, ignorance has locked the gate; the only key that opens it is love."

In a real sense, silence is the wisest value a rishi possesses, because it needs no arguments to persuade. In the presence of a rishi, the listener becomes like a rishi himself. This is not a delusion. Everyone possesses the rishi value — the capacity for wisdom — at the quietest level of his consciousness. When it senses its likeness, it simply responds.

Like speaks to like, and not all our problems can stand in the way. Once a person has done all he can to help himself using the power of his muscles, his words, and his intellect, he finds himself still attached to his problems. He may not recognize them yet. Like the dull *sadhu*, he needs to meet Kabir. If he really has met Kabir, then the steps ahead are easy. Anxiety rises to oppose him, but on the other side is a powerful silence. It breaks the attachment to problems and allows Nature to provide its own remedies. It takes life as it comes. If that silence is innocently cultivated, using no effort or struggle, then its power will increase until ignorance and disease disappear. Human life becomes much simpler once we find the silence that is Nature's heart.

Since the name Kabir did not satisfy my entire family, we named the new baby Gautama. It, too, is an old name. It was given to the ancient prince who attained enlightenment ages ago as the Buddha. Everyone in the family thought it was an auspicious choice, and my relations were sure that it showed a respectable parentage for our son. Anybody would recognize that Gautama was not found. We also introduced him, as we did Mallika, to meditation from a very young age.

Now that he is eleven, Gautama knows much more of inner silence than children before his generation. He does not need to have reality restored, because he is enjoying one that is in full bloom. And since he has known no other way, his trust in his own awareness is very strong. I encourage him to believe that he can accomplish anything. His thoughts are inquiring and happy, and already he can remain absorbed for hours in a book. He also says surprising things.

When Gautama was eight, he used to sit transfixed by the evening news. One night he was watching a presidential news conference while I was dressing.

"How's it going?" I asked him.

"I think he has matured a lot this year," Gautama said.

Another time, when he had crawled into bed with me so I could tell him a story, he said, "We're having fun this time, aren't we?"

"Oh, have we met before?" I joked.

He thought for a second. "Yes," he said seriously, "I remember us on a bridge in Tibet. There were tall mountains behind us, but we were in a valley. You were an old man with a gray beard, and we shared a bowl of rice together." He talked quietly to me, spinning his tale, and I was happy to watch his affectionate eyes. With a sudden, small pang, I realized, just then, that Gautama lives in the land of Kabir. He is my boy, but he is also the child of his own stillness. It is older than two old men on a bridge in Tibet. I think of how lucky Gautama is, to know freedom and love so effortlessly. The rishi value in his awareness is a living reality to him. What assistance Nature will bring to him, he can freely accept, without anxiety. Trust is not strange to him, so I know he will be welcomed by life as few people my age have been.

He will grow up close to Nature's heart.

11

The Art of Being

THE HAPPIEST PERSON I know right now is two years old. Her name is Priya, and she is the daughter of some Indian friends. Priya comes over my doorstep in a gust of gladness. She is so pleased with herself! She plays with my heart like a puffball. The last time she came to visit, she noticed that we had a new carpet. Her eyes widened.

"Who's that?" she pealed. "I love her!" And she could hardly keep from falling down, she laughed so hard. I noticed that she had on new shoes, little girl's black patent leather shoes.

"Priya," I said, "you have shiny shoes."

"Because they're happy shoes," she told me. Everything Priya looks at reflects one light of happiness. When her glass of milk was set down on the table, she cried, "Oh, I love her!" And she leaned over to kiss the rim. Nothing is not alive to her just now. I showed her a soft chair in the living room, and she said, "Who's she?" And naturally she laughed as she said it.

When Priya is like this, she reminds me of Sir Thomas Browne. There are not many doctors who are also poets, but

Sir Thomas Browne was one. He coined a telling phrase, "the inexhaustible laughter of Heaven." I think he is exactly right. Our laughter is inexhaustible if we can find it, and it comes directly from heaven. Sir Thomas also meant that heaven was inside ourselves, because in another place he said, "There is surely a piece of divinity in us, something that was before the elements, and owes no homage unto the sun."

Priya's mother is a little worried that her daughter looks at rugs, glasses, and chairs as if they were alive. I am forced to resort to doctor talk, explaining that Priya is going through a perfectly normal stage of childhood development. But secretly I think something different. I think she is in bliss. "Bliss," or what the Vedas call *ananda*, is a permanent attribute of the self. There are two others, *sat* and *chit*, which mean "immortality" and "consciousness." When Maharishi says that man is *sat chit ananda*, eternal bliss-consciousness, he simply means that we have always been conscious and always will be. And we will always be in the utmost joy, in bliss. We own the inexhaustible laughter of heaven. We are free.

Maharishi, of course, did not invent this formulation, *sat chit ananda*. It can be found in the oldest texts of the Indian tradition, beginning with the *Rig Veda*. But Maharishi has taken it from books and translated it into a living reality through TM. In the West we all tend to assume, unquestioningly, that we are made happy by events outside ourselves. If happiness is inside our essential nature, we do not often realize it. We would worry if we were as happy as Priya. In Nietzsche's famous phrase, man is the only animal who has to be encouraged to live. But the Eastern view holds that happiness is an attribute of our eternal selves. Being separate from the body and finer than the mind, it owes no homage under the sun. It resides in our piece of divinity.

The beauty of this view is that it makes permanent happiness possible. Instead of chasing after the next stimulus that will arouse happiness, one contacts Being, the fundamental level of the self. This is the technique of meditation. Over and over, Maharishi has emphasized that it is absolutely necessary to contact Being. We glimpse it, just briefly, in the silent gaps between our thoughts and in bursts of enjoyment that spring up in ourselves, but the systematic method is meditation. Its purpose is to expose the mind repeatedly to the source of happiness and then allow it to be carried over into activity, like a diver coming out wet from the water. Maharishi has said that the amount of happiness in a person's life is simply the amount of bliss he has brought out from Being into the active waking state.

That is the classic Indian view, rubbed free of encrustations. It is wisdom made bright and simple. The art of Being *is* simple, far simpler than thoughts about it or words on the page. If anything, the great challenge for a rishi is to convince others that the highest path requires no complexities. You meditate and then enjoy. It seems so labored to call Maharishi a sage, though he is preeminent as one. He has both the wisdom of the cosmos and the joy of Priya.

The proof of his words is seen in those who have listened. The only group of truly happy people I have ever encountered are TM meditators because, first of all, they have grasped the truth of the inexhaustible bliss inside our being. Second, they reach the self through meditation and therefore have a new infusion of *ananda* every day.

Dr. Triguna has expressed a high opinion of the health he finds in meditators. I have seen him hold a person's pulse and say, "You are laughing inside. You are a very funny man." He has not told that to those who do not meditate. He has also said that meditation is the greatest purifier of imbalances in the body. Here he speaks with the authority of the greatest Ayurvedic texts. Ayurveda prescribes hundreds of measures to prevent and control potential disease processes, but in a healthy person, meditation overrides all of them. Finding a way to happiness is medicine enough.

Because I heard them very young, it is easy for me to live with words like bliss and *ananda*, but I know that my patients — indeed, most people — find discomfort in such words. What are they comfortable with instead? They prefer to believe in deep suffering and fleeting joys. But even acute pain is a mask that falls away much more easily than people realize. I read of an incident recently where the mask slipped away quite unexpectedly. A man in Kansas City who was the usual successful type, very pressured and driving, was playing handball. Like everything else, he played the game tough. He took a particularly hard swing, lost his balance, and fell to the floor. As he went down, he distinctly heard his Achilles' tendon rip in two.

By any account, this is an agonizing injury. But the man realized only that he was laughing. He knew he should be feeling pain, but instead he felt overwhelming joy. He had fallen into *ananda*. As they carried him to the hospital on a stretcher, he kept on laughing. And he was still laughing when his family came to see him. Naturally, they thought he had lost his mind. The ways of the self can be peculiar. Sanity, in the form of joy, waits under the mask for only so long. Then it gets tired of toughness and pressure. It breaks out, and it doesn't care much if it has picked a socially embarrassing moment. This man thought his bliss would last forever. It didn't, and as the bliss was fading, he wrote down his story in part as a plea to find a way back to it. I hope meditation came his way. While his bliss lasted, the sky and the flowers, the trash can and the stray cats, were equally wonderful to him. They were all alive. They brought out in him the inexhaustible laughter of heaven.

I recently saw a patient who had been diagnosed three months earlier with terminal lung cancer. Then he happened to read a book in which I talked about spontaneous remissions, which are inexplicable and usually total recoveries from cancer.

Sometimes they occur by themselves, at other times in conjunction with standard therapies. They are quite rare in either case. No one can account for the mechanism that causes them, but nearly every doctor has witnessed one.

If a remission is going to occur, it does not matter how advanced the cancer is. One woman I treated had such a virulent and copious malignancy in her abdomen that we could not even operate. We took one look inside her and simply closed the incision. She received no further treatment. She recovered completely within less than a year. Spontaneous remissions are not polite to scientific medicine. They will not fit into our system of convenient explanations, but they will not go away, either.

This man with lung cancer called me from his home in California and asked me to see him. He was in his late forties and a heavy smoker. He told me that he agreed with me about the role of the self in health. If spontaneous remissions existed, he wanted one. His doctors had given him three months to live. They offered him a full course of treatment, including chemotherapy and radiation, but they doubted that any of it would help. He had squamous-cell cancer, a deadly type that drugs and radiation do not combat well. Since the treatment itself would create its own problems, the doctors advised him to go home and enjoy the time remaining to him.

I agreed to see him, though I knew he would be nearly untreatable. I was right. He brought his X-rays with him, but I hardly needed to look at them. I could see the swollen lymph nodes standing out from his chest and neck. The cancer had already spread. His lungs had collected fluid, which caused him to be uncomfortably short of breath. The X-rays showed large shadows, the masses of malignancy.

"Let's get you well," I said. He looked at me, at first with amazement, then with tremendous relief. He was beyond the art of medicine, and that had brought him despair. Now someone was introducing the art of belief. I considered his happiness at least as important as his survival. I described a schedule of diet, rest, meditation, and a special regimen called *panchakarma*, which Ayurveda uses to detoxify the body. *Panchakarma* literally means "the five actions," a routine of massage, herbal steam baths, and other measures that are quite effective if properly handled. I told him that *panchakarma* was not a cure, and its restorative effects were hard to explain by Western standards, but it has shown itself able to relieve pain and restore a sense of well-being, even in terminal illness. It sets the stage for the patient's own power to recover.

This power may become debilitated, but we never lose our connection to it. I explained to him that Ayurveda places its highest emphasis on allowing consciousness to find its own way through the damage in the body. His will to recover was the only starting point we had, but it was also the best. The lifelines were horribly tangled, but they were still lifelines. I also asked him to quit smoking. Nothing was said about a cure, but everything I said was positive.

Then I suggested that spontaneous remissions are motivated at the deepest level of the self and involve the desire of the whole person to recover completely. Guided by this uncompromising thought, the body has no choice but to obey. He and I, as physician and patient, must be convinced to the depths of our hearts that he was going to get well.

When he asked me outright how I would cure him, I evaded the question. "You're the player," I said. "My staff and I are only the cheerleaders. But we'll never stop cheering."

He listened to me quite eagerly. I asked if we could make a pact. He had to promise me to get well. He agreed. I could see that this simple tactic strongly affected him. We shook hands on it: he was going to recover from this cancer, and that was that. He left with a sense of purpose I had not seen in him an hour earlier. He might be happy again, even though his illness seemed to pose such a huge obstacle.

In evading the question about curing him, I was not playing him false — I was trying to steer his attention away from his disease toward the deeper reality that he had to contact if he wanted to recover. Many patients fear this reality, I have found, because it is unknown. They feel that whatever underlies their illness must be something very grim. Yet every tradition of wisdom tells us that the deepest reality is only happiness. Modern medical studies repeatedly show that being happy is excellent protection against illness. The positive emotions apparently set up a basic biochemistry in the nervous system that directly enhances the body's ability to ward off sickness and combat it when it appears.

I do not promote spontaneous remissions among cancer patients. But I am convinced that doctors hold inner beliefs that affect the course of their patients' illness. Even if the doctor says nothing to bring his feelings to the surface, the patient knows. There is no such thing as a value-free silence. I have even heard a new term, "nocebo," to match the well-known placebo. Nocebo is the belief that the patient is not going to get well. If the belief is strong enough, the inevitable happens: there is no recovery. At best, the course of treatment follows the statistical averages. If the nocebo can be converted to placebo, however, to the belief that the patient *will* get well, then the inevitable disappears. I could see no clinical evidence that my lung cancer patient had much of a chance. I could also see that he knew it.

The man went to a health center that Maharishi had asked me to set up outside Boston in 1985. There he experienced deep silence. He resumed his meditations — as it happened, he already knew TM. We gave him simple, fresh food, some special Ayurvedic teas, and a few exercises, and he began the routine of *panchakarma*. Word came to me that he was doing very well. His breathing was less forced. His skin tone, sleep, and digestion were improving. There was promise of a growing inner confidence, and he continued to outlive his doctors' original expectations, week by week. I didn't see him myself, however, because every time I showed up, he was not around. It was strange. I could be walking down the corridor in his direction, and as soon as he saw me he would duck another way.

One night I went late from my practice to the health center and noticed this man walking down the street nearby. My curiosity got the better of me. I followed him to a convenience store. He approached the counter, bought a pack of cigarettes, and walked behind the doughnut rack. Before I left, I watched him smoke three cigarettes in a row. He didn't see me.

The next time I caught up with him, I asked how he was doing. Great. I asked if he was going to get well. Absolutely. We talked for a while, and he seemed not quite sincere. As he was leaving, as gently as I could, I asked him if he was still smoking. He said that he now smoked hardly at all. I asked him when he had smoked his last cigarette. He didn't remember. Could he guess? At that, he sat back down. I could see that he was very upset. He began to cry bitterly.

I told him that I really didn't care if he smoked. After all, he already had lung cancer. And he didn't have to feel guilty to please me. It was just our pact I wondered about. Did he really believe that he was going to get well? It was a difficult and cathartic moment for this man, and he went through unexpected emotions. He kept repeating that he knew he was going to get well. But I thought we might be facing a wall.

It was a delicate situation. Talking to him about getting well was like committing a cruelty. Perhaps, as his doctor, I could make myself believe in getting him well, but I didn't know the same from him. His actual belief was an imponderable. As I watched him agonize, he gave me the impression of being caught up in the long habit of struggling. Most of us are taught that life is a struggle, after all. He must have struggled more than once with his smoking. Now he was struggling with a fatal disease. He thought he was doing the right thing. But it wasn't helping him because it was just more of the same.

"You know," I told him, "a completely recovered person is already there, inside you. It's your real self, just waiting to be found." His face showed disbelief, the impact of a new idea. I was sure that a part of him already knew the truth, anyway. Getting well does not need struggle. There is no enemy within. Recovery for him lay only at the level of Being. If he contacted the self, it could pull him away from the brink.

It was a lot to ask of anyone. He left me still troubled. What I feared for him was that he didn't fully want to recover. That is the ugliest part of sickness. One yearns for regeneration, but at the same time one fears it. Learning to overcome this fear requires insight. The patient must learn to look as deep as the first impulse that quickens his mind and breath. He must find his own Being. It does not lie with his body or his beliefs. These change and eventually pass away. The self alone is beyond change. It is perfectly healthy and happy in its own nature. It knows nothing of dread. It only wants to be.

At the same time that I was dealing with this patient, a woman called me from Oregon to express an interest in Ayurveda. She complained of chronic fatigue. She had learned TM and practiced the TM-Sidhis, but she felt that perhaps her body was not responding properly to them. When she consulted a doctor, he heard a heart murmur that sounded rather suspicious. He advised her to have an echo cardiogram, a harmless test that uses ultrasound waves to take a picture of the heart.

The woman had always considered herself healthy and avoided doctors, but she reluctantly had the test done. It disclosed that she had an atrial septal defect. The atria are the chambers of the heart itself, and the septum is the wall of muscle that divides them, left from right. In her case, there was a small hole in the septum. Blood was being pushed from one side of her heart to the other, causing the murmur. In time, because each heartbeat was leaking blood into the wrong cavity, complications would arise. She was sent to a cardiologist, who recommended that the hole be repaired. That meant surgery.

Out of the blue, after reading in a book what I had said about the role of positive attitudes in preserving health, she chose to consult me on this problem. She didn't want to give up thinking of herself as healthy, and she knew she shouldn't have surgery, despite the cardiologist's advice. Could she try Ayurveda instead? Would herbs and *panchakarma* help?

I felt uncomfortable advising someone I had never met over the phone, even though she and her husband repeated several times that they had complete faith in my judgment. I said that I thought the surgery was a good idea. They sounded disappointed, so I asked them to send me her records. They promised to do so immediately, and in the meantime they were going to see a second cardiologist. The woman's records came and told me just what she had reported. The heart defect was giving her only mild chronic fatigue now, but if it was allowed to go untreated, serious heart disease and even death could ensue.

When the couple called again, I told her that I felt she should undergo surgery. The second cardiologist had said the same thing. I tried to reassure her about the procedure. Even though it involved opening the heart, the chances of success were very high. Children were routinely given this operation to avoid future problems before they occurred. Fewer than 1 percent of patients suffered serious complications afterward. But I only made her more indecisive. In the course of a week she saw several more doctors and called me up repeatedly to say that she didn't want the surgery. Finally it came to a head.

"You are the only doctor I trust," she declared. "If you tell me to go ahead, I will." She still wasn't my patient, but I told her to have the surgery. Within a few days her husband called me with shattering news. His wife had developed a rare complication immediately after the operation. Despite large doses of anticoagulants, a blood clot had formed at the site of the surgery. Within a few hours it detached, moved through the arteries to her brain, and caused a massive stroke. She now lay in a coma. Her doctors could not detect that her pupils responded to light. They feared the worst. Her husband could hardly bring himself to tell me these things.

It was unbelievable to me. I was so shocked that all I could think to say was, "She's going to recover. We'll do it." I had never said such a thing before. It must have been a flash of sanity.

The husband went along at once. "What can we do?" he implored.

His wife was beyond both the art of medicine and the art of belief. We would have to start on the art of Being.

Since he and his wife were both meditators, I said that we would go back to the self. We would simply know that she was going to recover, fully. I would have her in my attention when I went to bed at night, just before falling asleep. I asked her husband to do the same. But the key thing would be contacting the self through meditation. Nature is the curer of all illness. What is Nature but our own nature? If we were in touch with that, at the purest level, then there could exist no other desire but that his wife should get well.

These were the words that just came out. But after we finished talking, I felt that I had said what I knew to be true. At the level of Being, this woman had the ability to recover completely. There was no reason that the impulse of healing should not make it up to the light.

The husband called the next day with the first good news. His wife had come out of her coma, but the damage had been grave. Her right side was entirely paralyzed, and she had aphasia, which meant that she could not speak. The doctors, who before this thought she might die, now said that she was unlikely to regain her speech or the feeling in her right side. I asked the husband to keep me posted, and in a day he had more encouraging news. According to her doctors, his wife's aphasia was expressive and not receptive. That meant that even though she could not speak, she could hear and understand words perfectly well. I asked him to tell her what we were doing and to fix her attention on getting well.

More news came to me in bits and pieces all that week. Every time, the situation sounded better. The husband told me happily that his wife could understand what we were doing. Her aphasia and paralysis both started to get better. Within two weeks, she was up and in a wheelchair. Less than a week later, she was walking again, and her speech sounded only slightly slurred. Elated, her husband told me that he expected her full recovery now. The doctors, he said, were astonished.

I did not have much time to react to all of this. My lung cancer patient went into a crisis at just that time. His forced breathing suddenly became severe — he seemed to be smothering in the effusions of his lung fluid. I rushed to help and successfully alleviated each episode, but he had reached a turning point. When the crisis ended, he looked very happy. In a short while, however, he began to feel angry and restless. He kept up his smoking. His daughter finally came to me and said that he wanted to go home. I consented, sadly pointing out that in many respects he was responding quite successfully. He had come to our clinic after doctors predicted he would live only four months; now it had been eight. Perhaps there would be more. He decided to leave anyway. Since then, more than a year has passed. The daughter would have contacted us, I think, if her father were still alive.

The woman in Oregon sent me a letter a few weeks after I last talked to her husband over the phone. How long had it taken her to recover from her stroke? Six weeks, I figured. The aphasia must also be completely gone if she could write a letter. I felt very happy for her. The letter was infused with a sense of relief. It ended by saying that she still wanted Ayurvedic treatment. This time, I urged her to come.

This case marked a change in my psychology that has progressively deepened since then. In my eyes, a good doctor had always been someone who accepted his patient without reservation, who could be dispassionate in the face of any disease, no matter how ugly, and understanding of any behavior, no matter how distorted by pain.

But this woman and I, who had never seen one another, did not meet on the level of disease or even personality. Something deeper had been stirred. We still played the same roles, in the sense that she was the patient asking me as physician for help. This time, however, she had asked in silence, and out of silence I had answered. It was as if a river of compassion ran beneath our feet, and unable to reach down for herself, she had asked me to reach for her.

We were bound by emotions that lie beyond personality. We were bound by love. A patient occupies a privileged position in my life that nothing else can explain. Such profound feelings occur only when the physician is totally willing to accept his responsibility. If there is any fear of disease, any rejection of the patient, or any clinging to authority, then conventional medicine cannot be transcended. What should be an art remains a common trade.

More and more, I believe that the transcending can happen because I have come to feel, when I am face to face with patients, that I *am* them. I lose the sense that we are separate. We are not. I can feel their pain as they describe it. I can understand them without blame and want them to get well because I will be getting well myself.

This intimacy has grown very close in the last few years, but it does not embarrass either me or them. It is a very simple equation, really, one that is part of natural medicine. It only requires me to feel that I am a doctor, not just someone who has put on the mask of doctor. "He who wants to do good knocks at the gate; he who loves finds the gate open." This line, from the great Bengali poet Rabindranath Tagore, is my new standard for a good physician.

These two cases show that medicine is severely limited in its ability to cure. But the encouragement is that there is a deeper level from which cure can arise. The techniques for contacting this level deserve to be known and taught to patients. If the doctor will listen, the rishi can tell him something: before the art of medicine comes the art of belief, but before either comes the art of Being.

12

The Ashoka Pillar

ONE AUNT OF MINE we rarely saw when I was growing up. She was a quiet woman whose sweetness we all loved, but her visits to our house were never long. Her life was spent in religion, and alone. She had no husband, a tragedy for an orthodox woman in India. Her name was Kamla; all the children called her Kamla Auntie.

When she was just a girl, something extraordinary happened to Kamla. A marriage had been arranged for her with a man in the military. The wedding took place, but then he decided that she was not suitable — I never knew why. He had the marriage annulled, took a wife more to his liking, and sent Kamla away. Custom rigidly forbade her to remarry. My father, who was her brother, was indignant that someone should treat his sister in this way, and he took the army officer to court. Kamla Auntie moved to Lucknow and became a devotee of the temples and the sacred singing called *kirtan*. It suited her nature, actually. Her personality was innocent and beautifully spiritual.

Kamla Auntie was pregnant when the officer sent her away. She gave birth to a son, whom she named Ashoka, after the greatest warrior king of India. For some reason, all of us called him Koki.

As Koki grew up, we saw much more of him than of his mother. He visited his father only once a year and often came to our house on school vacations rather than return to his mother. You cannot expect a boy to be very interested in temples. With us he could play cricket and hockey or go for a swim. I admired Koki incredibly. In my eyes he had every blessing. He was four years older than I and a champion at all our games. Like his namesake and his absent father, he was going to become a soldier. He had been sent away to the Modern School, the finest place for boys in New Delhi. This had been mandated by the courts, thanks to my father's suit. The judge ruled that if Koki's absent father would not raise him, he should at least be obliged to pay for the finest education for him.

Koki was a star at school. He excelled in his studies, he won all the ribbons in sports. I was terribly excited whenever he came to see us. Our whole family accepted him as a son and brother. In time, Koki graduated to the National Defense Academy, which is the Indian equivalent of West Point, though run entirely on the British system. He continued to be brilliant. He won the sword of honor, the highest distinction for a cadet, and was one of the very youngest commanders of a cadet brigade. I couldn't imagine anyone finer. No one in our family had a kind word for his father, naturally, but Koki managed to befriend even him. I think he admired his father for his military virtues, but Koki may have loved him.

I was particularly thrilled when Koki came to see us in his full-dress cadet uniform. He looked as dashing as a general, and every night he went to the Delhi nightclubs, his black hair as perfect and polished as his regimental boots. Koki also knew how to rhumba. He would come home very late and wake me up.

"You know what, Deepak?" he invariably said, "I danced the rhumba with *twenty* girls." I found this incredible. I held on to his hand while he told me every detail. I could imagine the twenty girls, all beautiful, with queen-of-the-night blossoms entwined in their glossy hair. They were demurely sipping their pomegranate juice or mango *lassi* after the rhumba. They might even shyly peek at the chest of Koki's uniform, where so many medals would one day hang, all the medals the Indian army could stamp out. They would have never dared to inquire about the horrors of battle. Since he was still only a cadet, Koki of course had never heard a shot fired in anger. He studied old Sandhurst manuals in his classes, according to tradition. Probably, if Waterloo had had to be fought again, the cadets would have known precisely how to do it.

I saw much less of Koki after I went to medical school. He graduated from the academy about the time I went away. News would come to me that his career was turning out to be an illustrious one. He rose rapidly. The young lieutenant became a young captain, then a young major, a colonel, finally a brigadier, before he turned forty. But our paths did not cross again until the sixties, during the Indo-Pakistani war, when Ashoka got his chance on the battlefield.

Koki was a captain when hostilities broke out. The war grew out of a stale argument — a long-disputed strip of land in Kashmir that both sides had claimed since independence in 1947. We were all for the fight when it started. Feelings in India then were incredibly jingoistic. Considering our legacy from Gandhiji, we were shamelessly exhilarated by our war and the hatred we generated toward Pakistan. We even avoided old friends who had Moslem names. The streets of Delhi were spitting with vicious talk.

Koki wound up with his company at the front lines. They were holed up in a mountain village facing a Pakistani company across the river. His mission was to raid the enemy and secure the village. For a while, both sides waited without making a move. The decisive moment had not yet come. To judge by the bottles of rum that the soldiers drank all night, a question of courage might have been involved. To keep up a show of belligerence, the opposing sides would scream horrible insults at each other from behind the barricades. They also got a chance to do this face to face, since both sides had to visit the same fields in the morning — Kashmiri villages do not have indoor plumbing. The taunts always ended with one soldier yelling, "You're done for now, cowards! The captain has ordered a raid tonight. You're gone!"

The night had to come when Koki did in fact order a raid. The men were terribly frightened. Even the young officers had never experienced battle outside training exercises. They drank rum all that night and charged at dawn. The battle plan came straight out of the Sandhurst manuals, proper strategy from the age of muskets. But now each side had machine guns. The casualties ran gruesomely high: after a few hours, 90 percent of the Pakistani troops were killed or wounded and about 60 percent of the Indians. At the climax of the gunfire, the company commanders met each other face to face. The Pakistani captain had been wounded in the abdomen. Koki had a cluster of shrapnel in his thigh. Both were on the verge of collapse. They still had a chance to kill each other, but the Pakistani knew he had lost and managed to tell Koki that he was surrendering. Then the two captains dropped to the ground from their wounds.

When the news came to our family in Delhi that Koki was in serious condition and being flown to the city for treatment, we were extremely worried. For six hours we did not know if he was dead or alive. At that point, I did not feel much like a war hero anymore. The medical students had been looked upon as heroes of a sort. We were organized into rescue squads of about ten, each headed by a professor. As it happened, my squad commander was also a military officer, a Colonel Kalra. He had made his mark in medicine during the Second

World War when he spotted an unknown type of rickettsial disease while fighting on the front in Burma, the same theater of war where my father served. Now Colonel Kalra was a world-recognized authority on such diseases, and the students had tremendous respect for him.

The medical squads were assigned air raid duty. Indian jets were dropping bombs over Lahore, the capital of Pakistan, so retaliation was expected from its air force. When the raids came, we were to take shelter in ditches outside our dorms — they served, not too well on the whole, as civilian protection. As soon as the raid was over, the squad would proceed posthaste to join Colonel Kalra in the sector of the city assigned to us, where we would take care of the wounded and search the rubble for casualties. On no account was anyone to stay in his room when the sirens sounded, since that was considered the most dangerous place to be during a raid.

At last, after some tense days of waiting, the first air raid came. It was near sunset when I became aware of a faint droning sound in the sky. It seemed insignificant, but I turned a little queasy. My neighbor, the student in Room 3, instantly began screaming at the top of his lungs — a piercing, completely uncontrolled shriek. I was suddenly so terrified, I immediately crept under my bed. We now could hear the *ack-ack* of the anti-aircraft guns on the perimeter of New Delhi. The droning grew louder. I couldn't even tell what was happening to me. I clasped my hands and trembled, and when it was all over I was sobbing. I didn't know why. No bombs had fallen at all.

Almost none of the students had gone to the ditches for shelter. We now massed outside the buildings and began to jump up and down, full of ire. We shook our fists at the skies. We hurled incredible insults at the departing Pakistani jets. War heroes. Then someone said, "What about Colonel Kalra?" We had forgotten all about him.

The ten of us assigned to his squad grabbed our flashlights

and ran off into the night, toward the sector where Kalra had expected us an hour earlier. When we arrived, we found him sitting on the ground, making little sketches of microbes in a notepad. He looked very intent. Apparently this was what he had been doing throughout the raid. He looked up at us and smiled.

"Oh, I think you must be late, boys," he said. He was quite a kind man. "It doesn't matter. Just sit down here. I will tell you some more about rickettsia. It is really so fascinating."

Colonel Kalra was absolutely in love with microbes. For our part, we loved to hear him talk about them. We sat around with our flashlights, forgetting the time, while he discoursed. He talked about the bloody campaign in Burma, where months at a time were passed in rain, forced marches, and close fighting. He turned to the incidence of Rocky Mountain spotted-tick fever, which falls under his specialty, and gave us clinical details until the dawn came. The air raids continued for a while, and in the future our squad obeyed its orders better, but we never found any rubble or any wounded to treat.

The two captains who were flown to Delhi by helicopter recovered from their wounds, and the Pakistani became Koki's prisoner. They were both put into the same recovery ward in the military hospital, and after a while there, they hit it off. The two of them would sit up through the night in their bandages, playing cards or carom, a favorite board game in India. Whenever my mother brought sweets for her nephew, she naturally included his friend. Their grimmer memories of combat began to fade, and Koki found it amusing to tease the Pakistani about his surrender of the Kashmiri village. The other captain would try to tease him back, but he preferred just to play cards.

When the time came for the Pakistani captain to return home, our whole family accompanied him to the airport. This would be the last we heard or saw of him. As they embraced in farewell, he and Koki lingered. They did not want to let go of each other. One began to cry, then the other, and in a minute they were both sobbing with unpent emotion, wounded enemies in the Delhi airport. The strain of living in hatred had to break, and it broke first between comrades.

But it was certain nonetheless that the captain would walk back into exactly the same atmosphere of war and the same insane animosity that he had left behind in Lahore. The streets of Pakistan ran with the same poisoned talk. A Hindu name made you a traitor there, as a Moslem one did here. Members of our family who hardly knew the Pakistani captain started to cry now. I felt like crying, too.

Kamla Auntie had named her baby son after a famous warrior king, but not so that he would lead men into battle. The emperor Ashoka is revered in India for bringing an era of universal peace. After conquering an empire that extended beyond India into the regions of Nepal, Kashmir, and Afghanistan, Ashoka looked back on the carnage he had caused and felt a deep remorse. He had made himself a king of strife. He immediately resolved to find enlightenment for himself and his subjects and was instructed in the path of the Buddha. The word "path" brings personal salvation to mind, but Ashoka was actually seeking freedom from suffering and conflict in a completely practical sense. He had himself and an empire to rid of ignorance. Through meditation and knowledge of the truth, he reached his goal and became Ashoka the saint. The remainder of the warrior king's life was devoted to the rule of justice and mercy.

Along the highways of his empire, he had way stations placed where travelers could rest. Water and fruit were handed to them by emissaries of the emperor. The roads everywhere became safe to travel. Ashoka decreed that iron pillars be erected throughout India, proclaiming the simple rules of conduct that would keep his people peaceable. His delegates carried Buddha's truth as far east as China and Japan, where Ashoka pillars were also erected. When his golden age ended, the pillars at least would endure.

And some have. One still stands outside Delhi. People travel there to embrace it in the belief that anyone who is able to put his arms around an Ashoka pillar and join fingers on the other side can make a wish and have it come true. The iron is more than two thousand years old, but it still looks bright. Some unknown and remarkable alloy went into it, and the touch of so many embraces helps keep away the rust.

This pillar is not as high as it once was — its top has been chopped off, no one knows how long ago. Any tall man now stands higher than it does. But the writing in Pali is still legible. It repeats the way of self-respect, love, and nonviolence that led Ashoka to find his own peace. An enlightened voice speaks from his pillar, telling us that men are destroyed by their own anger.

In the absence of enlightened emperors, we have to raise our own Ashoka pillars. Here again, some unexpected principles come into play. Late in 1974, a new finding was brought to Maharishi's attention by TM researchers. Statistics from four American cities where 1 percent or more of the population were practicing TM showed that the crime rate had dropped by a significant percentage. At that time, the national crime rate was rising, and it would be difficult to account for why these cities in particular had reversed the trend.

Maharishi predicted as early as 1960 that meditation could influence the environment. He cited the Vedic texts, which declare that enlightened men bring peace to their surroundings simply through the *sattva*, or purity, of their consciousness. Perhaps this was the onset of such an effect, he suggested. Intrigued and excited, the researchers went away to make more observations.

In the mid-seventies, TM had entered a boom period, with

twice as many new people learning the technique every year, so one could find a number of cities, including Boulder, Colorado, and Berkeley, California, where 1 percent or more of the population had been taught. A 1976 study using eleven of these cities, conducted by the psychologist Dr. Candice Borland, revealed that their crime rate had dropped by as much as 16 percent in one year compared to the national rate, which was still rising.

Maharishi was delighted, and since he had been the originator of the explanation for this phenomenon, it was called "the Maharishi effect." Over the next decade, sociologists and statisticians around him were kept busy verifying that the Maharishi effect was valid. The original results have now been duplicated in many other towns and cities in the United States and abroad. According to outside review panels, the methods of analysis are scrupulously accurate, and study after study has come to one conclusion: as more people meditate, the negative tendencies in society decline. Statistical accuracy, however, can only carry you so far in science. Many outside observers were skeptical that a cogent explanation had been found.

The explanation offered by the rishis is simple: human consciousness is a whole, a single awareness that at a deep level is shared by all. This collective consciousness unites people at their source, and whatever is generated from there is accepted as our reality. When the collective consciousness is weak and in conflict, negative trends predominate in society: there is crime, war, and absence of knowledge about enlightenment. By the same token, if collective consciousness can be made more positive, these trends will decrease. It is just a matter of injecting a harmonious influence at the appropriate level, and everyone will feel the benefits.

In an earlier book, I have written a detailed explanation of how the mechanics of this might work. The TM scientists have offered explanations in terms of field theories from physics that are very enticing. The basic principle is like that of a laser. Normally, light is emitted as scattered, or incoherent, waves. But when light is generated in a laser, a small number of photons are aligned coherently, forming uniform waves, and their influence is enough to trigger a huge outpouring of coherence in all the other photons. The result is a laser, which is just coherent light moving in unison. Laser light is much more powerful than normal light: it can cut through steel or travel to the moon and back without losing focus.

As applied to meditation, the theory is that thoughts are also incoherent and weak in the usual waking state, but that meditation makes them more coherent by hundreds of times. (In fact, researchers have demonstrated strong brain wave coherence through TM which was unknown before the technique was studied.) By the power of coherent mental functioning, the meditators have an influence on the whole of collective consciousness, just as a few photons do for the whole laser beam. As a result, coherent awareness increases in general, and the most incoherent behavior among people — crime and war — is defeated at its source.

I was explaining this to a senior Democratic congressman in Washington one day. I had gone to see him primarily to introduce Ayurveda, but my theme touched on how the benefits of meditation might be shared in society. I was just on the point of defining collective consciousness, which people ordinarily find a little difficult to grasp, when the congressman interrupted me in midsentence.

"Doctor," he said, "what you're really trying to tell me is that at a very deep level, at the deepest level, we are all connected." I agreed.

"What you are saying further," he continued, "is that this is the reason why we are interested in each other, why I am affected by a hijacking in the Middle East even though I have no relatives on that plane. But I feel sorry and angry when I see that. This is the reason why my children give up lunch money so it can be sent to Ethiopia and another child can have a meal. It is the basis of our love for each other."

Touched by his words, neither of us said anything for a moment.

"If by some means,'" he went on, "we could be aware of this level, where we are really all one and the same, then hostilities would just disappear."

He had grasped the central point and brought it down to earth. If human beings can connect, then the sympathy that binds us will have an effect. The Maharishi effect is just an extension of this idea, based on far more powerful mechanics than sympathy.

From a physician's viewpoint, I take it that Maharishi's approach to peace is basically physiological. In India there has long been a value called *ahimsa*, nonviolence. This is commonly understood as the ethical refusal to harm others, even when provoked. But Maharishi places *ahimsa* much deeper. "What is the source of violence?" he asks. It must be violent thoughts and aggressive desires. Only if these can be eliminated will *ahimsa* be real. At bottom, Maharishi contends, violent thoughts and desires are just stress. If the nervous system were purified of stress, then it would only express Being, which is always life-supporting because its nature is bliss.

Meditation creates the true ground for nonviolence, since it systematically removes stress from the nervous system. A person whose nervous system is permanently devoid of all negative influences radiates only positivity into his environment. Therefore, he has become a unit of world peace. As more people reach this state, peace will spread. When there are enough of them, it will be permanent.

Maharishi has presented his method for creating peace at many press conferences. It is the main goal of his work, even under the name of Ayurveda. He says that a system of health must take care of the world as much as the individual. Who wants to be healthy, or even enlightened, in a miserable world?

One of his favorite themes is this: peace in the world is just a reflection of health in the family of nations. I have noticed that reporters will respond favorably to these terms. At a certain point, however, they balk and ask skeptically, "How are you going to stop an enemy who has bullets? Bullets are real, and so are atom bombs and missiles. Do you intend to stop them with your eyes closed? Come on."

This is like the doctor who believes that only the hardware of medicine is real. The best answer is to demonstrate that the Maharishi effect works. Once, in 1985, a military officer came to a private briefing arranged for him by TM teachers in Washington, D.C. He listened patiently to their plan for creating world peace, which consisted of establishing large groups of meditators to radiate coherence into the collective consciousness. He seemed interested. He was even open-minded enough to concede that the superpowers have virtually no ability to avert a catastrophic exchange if nuclear war breaks out. When the presentation paused, the officer leaned back, and a surprising thing happened.

He gave his opinion that the theory should be tested. The TM people said it had been, numerous times. And it worked? Always. You verified it statistically? Every time, to an accuracy better than one in ten thousand, often one in a hundred thousand — it wasn't random. And you eliminated the possibility that conventional causes were at work? Yes.

It was an interesting moment, because, as it happened, the officer worked in the Pentagon. He made it quite clear that he was not representing the Pentagon, but he was known to have influence there. Then he asked for specific examples of the Maharishi defense at work. Here are two:

One: A TM teacher whose parents lived in Lebanon feared for their safety. Their small village of Baskinta was in the war area under the most devastating bombardment from both sides. The surrounding mountains had been heavily armed with cannons during the past several years. TM's theory of collective consciousness held that if 1 percent of the people in the village meditated, they would not have to fear any enemy. So the teacher went home to Lebanon and taught TM to 1 percent of the villagers. Then he followed what happened to them. In the next six years the bombing increased, and the whole area was nearly demolished. Casualties and damage were horrendous. Not a single bomb fell on this village. One day a single shell hit a tree. Nothing was damaged and no one was hurt.

Two: During the Christmas holidays in 1983, enough meditators gathered in Fairfield, Iowa, to reach the number needed for a global effect, about seven thousand. They meditated together for two weeks to create strong waves of coherence in world consciousness and then left. During exactly that period, crime rates decreased in other countries, international hostilities cooled down, and even the stock markets rose on a global scale. The trends reversed when the assembly dispersed.

The officer didn't interrupt, and when the evidence had been laid out — in actuality, this took two hours to present fully and covered more than thirty experiments — he gave his considered opinion. It must be true, he said. You know how to create peace. But I can't help you. I know if I present these studies to an official review board, they will feel the way I am feeling now. At a certain point, everything seemed all right. But then something inside me snapped. You can stretch a man's belief system only so far before it snaps back farther than when you started. I feel afraid of what you are saying, so I am retreating. Good luck, anyway.

He was an astute man and an honest one. The sudden prospect of peace, like that of perfect health, can be scary. The TM people thanked him. It hadn't been a historic moment after all. But they were in a happy position, because they saw the next thing to do. They went to their rooms as usual and meditated.

I didn't meet Koki again for about twenty years, but I heard that his career continued to succeed. He wore a chestful of medals from the Indo-Pakistani war. He still walked with a limp from the shrapnel that was buried too near the bone to be removed. I also heard that he was married, with a son, and had become very spiritual. It came to me vaguely that his whole family had gone to visit a famous saint. This change in him didn't register with me, however. I still saw him as the cadet who danced the rhumba in nightclubs and told me about the twenty girls.

In 1985 I was back in New Delhi. At that time, my life was incredibly busy. I was a wanderer between my practice in Boston, Ayurvedic conferences in Washington, and an occasional dash to India, sometimes to talk to government officials, sometimes to visit Maharishi. More and more he remains in India, at home after thirty years of crossing oceans. On this visit, I spent considerable time at Maharishi Nagar, the site outside Delhi where Maharishi has centered his activities. In particular, I was consulting on a model Ayurvedic hospital that takes advantage of Maharishi's revival of the ancient knowledge in its purest form. He was incessantly occupied, spending twenty-hour days with the select vaidyas in whom he saw a real understanding of Ayurveda.

During the week, word came to me that Koki had flown in from the Himalayas. He had to rush back, but he absolutely needed to see me that night. Koki was a brigadier now. He commanded troops strung along most of the length of India's frontier with China. They were a key part of national defense. I wondered how long a string of Himalayan soldiers might last against a Chinese invasion.

We kept missing each other, and by evening I regretted losing my chance to see him. At the last minute, however, an army staff car showed up at our door. In India, a military staff car is a battered Ambassador with a droopy flag over the hood. The driver snapped to attention, and there was Koki. He really did have a chest entirely covered with medals. A great rush of affection swept over us, and we went up to my room and sat on the bed holding hands. I talked nonstop while Koki sat in silence. I was very full of the idea that meditation could be used for national defense.

"It is a tremendous thing," I kept saying. "If enough people meditate, it is impossible to have war. No enemy can arise to harm you at all." I knew what I was talking about, because the remarkable TM studies were fresh in my head.

Koki didn't say a word, but when I stopped, after about fifteen minutes, he seemed convinced.

"Then all my soldiers should meditate, shouldn't they," he said.

Time was running short. We had barely enough moments left to get him to his car so that he could make it to the military transport plane idling on the runway. He returned that night to his brigade based in Assam, far to the northeast of the capital.

I was surprised when he called again that night, at two in the morning. The telephone connection was impossible, and it was all I could do to hear a word.

"Hello?" I yelled into the phone.

"Tell me more about consciousness!" Koki yelled from his end. Something like that. He was apparently very excited by these new ideas.

"What? Hello?" I yelled back. It was ridiculous, but Koki kept calling me. I would come in from Maharishi Nagar, drop exhausted into bed, and again at two in the morning the call would come from Assam. Every time, I spent half the call yelling "Hello?" into the mouthpiece.

Koki must have heard me, though, because a large number of his soldiers did start to meditate. They became part of several large groups that Maharishi has inspired in India. It makes me feel hopeful for the future when people are willing to respond to enlightened thought in this way. The waves of coherence generated in silence can transform a world — men can still put their arms around Ashoka's pillar.

13

Flyers

I WASN'T THE OFFICIAL TIMEKEEPER, but I sneaked a peek at my watch anyway. Two minutes to go. The reporter sitting beside me stirred in his seat. Several television cameras stood in front of us, pointed at a small stage where six men, seated in lotus position, were meditating.

I was supposed to be meditating, too, so I closed my eyes again. One minute to go. The young woman on my right stood up. A bell rang. Without breaking the silence, we all looked toward the stage. Nothing happened. We waited, then all at once one of the men rose up about a foot into the air and bounded forward 4 feet, still in lotus. All the press cameras clicked, and the TV cameramen swiveled to follow him. The atmosphere in the room held a note of wonder — we were witnessing the first stage of human flight.

It was in the summer of 1986 that the Cambridge TM center asked me to explain "yogic flying" to the Boston press. I immediately agreed. The technique to move the body through the air at will, commonly called "levitation," has been taught by Maharishi since 1975, but for ten years no one had witnessed it publicly. Finally Maharishi had set a date, August 15, for demonstrations to be held in every major American city and many others abroad.

For our event, the recital hall of a music school had been rented in Cambridge, just a few blocks from the traffic snarl of Harvard Square. It was a pretty room, brightly lit by stage lights and the morning sunshine that came in through several large skylights. The stage was covered with 6-inch-thick pads of foam rubber. It had taken about thirty pieces to fill a space that a chamber orchestra for Mozart might comfortably fit in. A press release circulated the week before displayed a startling photo on the first page: two young men, arms outstretched and smiling, who seemed poised about 1½ feet in midair. We were confident of a good turnout.

The first liftoff sent a stir through the audience, but then the room turned quiet again. One after another, the six flyers bounded across the stage; the plopping sound as they landed sounded convincingly soft. A blond New Hampshire man whom the photographers seemed to like started to laugh as he hopped up in the air, and there was a fast flurry of shutters.

The young woman rang the bell again, signaling another five minutes of meditation. The flyers shut their eyes, and the audience, most of them meditators, joined them. Two men in stocking feet walked onstage from the wings and started to arrange foam pads two and three pieces high on one side. The next event was going to test how high our flyers could go. I felt a little uneasy. At the present stage of the technique, rising more than a foot into the air is a difficult challenge.

What we were doing in Cambridge was a follow-up to the "yogic Olympics," as the press dubbed it, which had been held in July in Washington, D.C. With about a thousand TM flyers to choose from, it was quickly evident that two or three contestants were in a class of their own. This was true both in America and in India, where the First International Yogic

Flying Competition had been held. The Indian events were plagued by spongy, thin foam, which is a misery to land on. The heat of Delhi in July had been oppressive, as usual, and the Indian press swamped over the competitors, making it difficult for the ten thousand spectators to see anything at all. However, they had been treated to a unique sight missing in the American competition: two hundred schoolboys from Maharishi Nagar hopping in formation, all bounding up and down to the rhythm of one inner impulse.

The press saw record hops of about 6 feet in length and 2 feet in the air. There were also events for speed. A star at these was Eddie Gob of Guadeloupe. In front of a hundred and twenty reporters in Washington, he won the sprints, hopping 50 meters across the foam, or about 150 feet, in 22.5 seconds. By comparison, the Wright brothers flew 120 feet at Kitty Hawk in 12 seconds.

Every demonstration had its own local flavor. In China, we were told, the event was booked into a Peking sports arena. A local official of the Communist Party handed out TM literature at the door, and as soon as the bleachers were full, two Chinese women TM teachers got on top of a Ping-Pong table to fly.

I knew we wouldn't set records in Boston, but we had found six adept flyers. When the bell rang again, they headed for the high jumps. All but one easily hopped onto the two-block platform, which was about 14 inches high. The flyers moved over to the higher jump, about 21 inches, but no one made it. Two flyers who had jumped it in practice rose high enough, their knees poised on the edge, but they fell back. The impulse to fly lasts for only a second at this stage of expertise and comes only at the instant of taking off. So once a flyer is airborne, he can't give himself a boost.

The bell rang again, signaling the end of the demonstration. The atmosphere in the hall changed totally, to relief and quiet exultation for the meditators, to various other emotions

among the press. The six flyers stood up and bowed to ac-
knowledge the applause. Each of them was handed a red rose
in thanks. I noticed the producer from the NBC affiliate staring impassively at the stage, a puzzled frown on his face. The
cameraman from public television, a tall black man, came over
to tell me how impressed he was. He said that he could feel
an impulse bubbling up inside him whenever one of the flyers
hopped. I was very pleased by this; such an experience is
usually observed only by meditators.

A young couple from Harvard came up to say that they
enjoyed the demonstration but liked the meditations best.
"How often do two hundred Americans sit still together in
one room for five minutes?" the woman remarked. The meditators in the hall who were not yet flyers and had never seen
yogic flying for themselves now exhibited the strongest reactions. I could see that they were very moved, some almost
to tears.

August 15 was a significant day for holding the demonstration of yogic flying since it is India's Independence Day. Maharishi has trained more than a thousand schoolboys in the
technique, and now they were being sent out in pairs to sev-
enty-eight cities throughout India. This was more than a
symbolic gesture. Although it is the home of yoga and of yogic
flying, India harbors many misunderstandings about it. As
in the West, yoga is confused with the physical postures that
belong to just one branch, hatha yoga.

Yoga literally means "union." It is the knowledge of attain-
ing the unity lying behind diverse experiences. The ancient
rishis compiled this knowledge working solely from their own
experiences. The data existed in their awareness, in the state
Maharishi calls pure subjectivity. One of the greatest rishis
was named Patanjali. His contribution was to write the *Yoga
Sutras*, a work usually translated as *Aphorisms of Yoga*. A better rendering, if less literal, would be *The Basic Formulas for*

Union. Exactly when Patanjali wrote his book has not been determined, but for many centuries the *Yoga Sutras* has been accepted as the canonical text for reaching enlightenment through yoga.

One section of the book is devoted to *sidhis,* or skills perfected in consciousness. Of the two dozen or more formulas that Patanjali records, one is for flying. It is just a single sentence, in which Patanjali declares that it is possible to fly through the air once the mind has been trained to maintain a state of deep meditation. From this one sentence, written before Western civilization had developed more than a rudimentary technology, Patanjali suggested another technology, based entirely on human awareness, which would make the work of Galileo, Newton, and Einstein pale by comparison. If he was right.

Those who think Patanjali was wrong have a remarkably weak position. Anyone can say that, of course, man cannot fly. But if the ability is demonstrated, even in the most primitive stages, then opponents really have no evidence to refute yogic flying simply because it makes absolutely no sense according to a Western scheme of reality. At best, the West admits flyers among its saints, such as St. Teresa of Avila, who was often seen in levitation by the sisters of her order. There are charming stories of how they were compelled to hold her down in the choir stall when the impulse to fly came during mass.

Teresa wrote of her experience: "Rapture is generally irresistible . . . it sweeps upon you so swift and strong that you see and feel yourself being caught up in this cloud and borne aloft as on the wings of a mighty eagle. . . . Even at times my whole body has been lifted from the ground."

As beautiful as her description is, no one in the West has systematically discussed the mechanics of flying. The science of consciousness, of which yoga is one prominent part, is India's legacy to human knowledge. It stands on its own premises, just as Western science does, and forms its own body of evidence and proof.

As it happens, the evidence and proof are there in abundance. After Patanjali recorded his aphorism on yogic flying, a famous commentary by another sage named Vyasa gave details of the technique that still hold true today. In fact, they must hold true if the experience of flying is valid, because the conditions that make it possible are unchanging. It does not matter when a person learns the technique of flying, or whether in Vedic India or contemporary America.

According to Patanjali and Vyasa, the person will first have to reach a state of completely even and balanced awareness through meditation; this is called *samadhi*. When he has meditated and reached this silent, even state, the person must next apply the mental technique that will allow him to lift up from the ground. The phrase "mental technique" simply means a correct thought. At first his body will not cooperate with the thought. If one sits in an armchair and thinks, "I want to fly," the body will not cooperate, but if the mind is in *samadhi*, there will be a result. The body will try to lift up; it will wriggle and grow hot or give other signs that a physical response is occurring. But the action is inefficient. It is rather like trying to multiply two four-figure numbers in your head — there will be effort in the right direction, but not the right result.

As the meditator continues to practice, he lays down a pattern of repetition in which the body more and more begins to understand what the mind wants. In scientific parlance this is called behavioral conditioning. In common language, he is acquiring a habit. Mundane as it sounds, flying is simply a habit. Over time, the body stops shaking and, unexpectedly, while doing nothing more than the same practice he has done in the past, the person accomplishes the result. His body lifts up and goes forward.

Needless to say, this is a remarkable moment for every

meditator, and of the fifteen thousand TM meditators in America who practice the yogic flying technique, each one remembers his first liftoff with incredible vividness. My own experience is probably fairly typical. I was sitting on a foam rubber pad, using the technique as I had been taught, when suddenly my mind became blank for an instant, and when I opened my eyes, I was 4 feet ahead of where I had been before. I felt the coldness of the foam where I had landed, my pulse raced into my temples, I felt my heart pound, and an unknown emotion flooded through me. It was a sense of the miraculous.

Lifting off, as it is called among meditators, is the first threshold in yogic flying. The ancient commentaries go on to describe flying in three stages, once the basic skill of lifting the body up through the power of intention has been acquired. The first is hopping, in which the body lifts up and goes forward a few feet. In this stage, the inner impulse that lifts the body into the air cannot be sustained. It comes in a flash and then is lost; therefore, the mind is thrown out of *samadhi,* and gravity immediately takes over with a jarring thump.

The second stage is hovering, usually called levitation, in which the meditator has grown so accustomed to reaching *samadhi* and using the flying technique that he can sustain the inner impulse. When a flyer has reached this stage, he can hold himself in the air at will, but several earlier signs will show that he is nearly there — he will find himself poised in the air for a second or two before he comes down, his liftoff will be gentle and his landing light, and he will come down slowly, like the landing of a thistledown instead of a rock.

The third stage is actual flying through the air at will. Even in India, where there are records and photographs of levitating saints, this third stage is regarded as all but mythical. One time in 1977, after Maharishi revived the flying technique in its correct form, the early experiences of hopping were being read at a press conference. The location was Seelisberg, Switzerland, where Maharishi had inaugurated scientific research into all advanced phenomena in the field of higher consciousness. The program to teach yogic flying had been named the TM-Sidhis, since it combined Transcendental Meditation with the abilities Patanjali called *sidhis*. At the time, Seelisberg was also the only place where the flying technique could be learned, and the little resort town above Lake Lucerne was flooded with meditators from the many countries where TM is taught. Now the technique is taught in several places throughout Europe, North and South America, and Asia.

Maharishi himself was present, listening silently as a young man read out experience sheets from flyers in England, New Zealand, and America. As he was reading one report from London, in which a young psychologist described flights of several seconds that took him 10 feet or more at a time, the young man at the press conference mentioned that naturally yogic flying would not be used as a means of transportation. We would still be taking buses and taxis. At this, Maharishi looked up and offered a correction. "Oh, no," he said, "we will fly outside the buses, even if just for fun."

When I spoke to the press in Cambridge, just before our flyers came out, I wanted to emphasize that yogic flying is not a physical feat, since Americans tend to see it as that.

"When you see these people go up in the air today," I said, "what you can do is photograph them and look at them as closely as you like. What you cannot see or take pictures of is what is going on deep inside them, where the real phenomenon is taking place. The yogic flying itself is superficial, an epiphenomenon. The unseen, real phenomenon is an experience of complete integration, combining mind and body. The technique operates through the central nervous system alone. Viewing it from the physiological perspective, it achieves maximum coherence in brain wave activity.

"I should give you the scientific definition of coherence,

since it is the most important term we use here. Coherence is a measure of the constancy of the relationship between brain waves at a particular frequency, as measured from different parts of the scalp. That's the scientific definition. But it is really a measure of the integration of the neurons everywhere in the central nervous system.

"A good analogy would be when you go to hear the Boston Symphony, and you arrive before the performance while the players are still practicing on their own as they tune up. Each performer is playing his instrument on the right notes, the right frequency, but the overall result is chaotic. There is no constancy in the relationship between the performers, and therefore what you get is noise. Once the performance starts, they are still playing the same notes on the same instruments, but there is a constancy of relationship — there is music. This constancy of relationship is coherence.

"When our yogic flyers lift off the ground, they have intense, peak brain wave coherence. What is even more interesting is that this brain wave coherence is not present only in the people who are doing the flying. It is also present, and can be measured, in the people who are in the surroundings. We are in the same atmosphere, so far as consciousness is concerned, and our brain wave coherence also goes up, even though we are not doing the yogic flying ourselves."

This point about brain wave coherence is extremely important to Maharishi's TM-Sidhis. In 1979, when meditators practicing the TM-Sidhis gathered for a conference in Amherst, Massachusetts, it was shown that their meditations strongly affected someone more than a thousand miles away. The experiment was simplicity itself. A meditator in Fairfield, Iowa, the site of Maharishi International University, was connected to an EEG, or electroencephalogram, and asked to meditate. He was not told the reason for the experiment or asked to do anything other than meditate normally. During the experiment, the group in Amherst began their sidhis program. When the EEG of the Iowa meditator was examined, the pattern of his brain waves was shown to alter exactly when the sidhis in Massachusetts began and ended exactly when they ended.

The researchers were showing that consciousness could display the attributes of a field extending in all directions, just as magnetic north affects a compass on any part of the earth's surface. I have already mentioned how the effect of meditation can lower crime rates in a given area. The scientists now demonstrated that the area does not have to be localized — the field of consciousness is global. The phenomenon looked like a more powerful version of the Maharishi effect, so it was named "the extended Maharishi effect." Computing how many people were needed to produce it, the scientists calculated that, instead of 1 percent of the population meditating, which was the threshold for the Maharishi effect, the extended Maharishi effect required only the square root of 1 percent. This represented an enormous decrease. For example, it would take more than forty million meditators to create the Maharishi effect for the whole world, but only seven thousand practitioners of the TM-Sidhis.

Maharishi commented that this jump in magnitude was predictable. Meditation dissolves stress, he said, but the *sidhis* smash through it. He had realized in the mid-seventies that stress was decreasing in those who had learned Transcendental Meditation; however, the stress of the world as a whole, as measured by overall negative trends, was still on the rise. Seeing that, Maharishi felt that peace could not be achieved even though the Maharishi effect worked. He decided to introduce the sidhis as a much more powerful technology.

After ten years of teaching the sidhis, Maharishi expressed satisfaction with the results. He felt that world peace was now a realistic goal. It required only one or two groups of seven thousand flyers to meditate from one location and radiate coherence into the collective consciousness of the world. He

turned his efforts to establishing such groups, and starting in
1985, he began to build a group around himself in India. So
far, the group in India has grown to more than three thousand, almost all of them the schoolboys Maharishi is educat-
ing in the Vedic knowledge at Maharishi Nagar.

Although his project to create world peace has proceeded
by logical, systematic steps, it falls on Western ears as du-
bious. A high school junior came to interview me about
Ayurveda a month ago, and I mentioned to him all the aspects of health that were involved, from physical and mental
to social and environmental. Ayurveda works through a much
deeper idea of the physiology than we think about, I said,
and so it is possible to say that world peace is actually a health
measure. It marks the decline of stress in the world, just as
good health marks the decline of stress in your own body.
The TM scientists studying the extended Maharishi effect have
also found that not just crime and war but infectious diseases
and hospital admissions decline whenever a large group per-
forms the TM-Sidhis together.

He listened attentively and went away to write his story
for the newspaper of the high school he attended in Belmont.
But a week later he came back. "I can accept everything you
told me," he explained, "but the flying part is too hard. Just
because you can do a little hop in the air doesn't mean you're
going to fly, does it?"

He was offering the instinctive objection to yogic flying.
Not that it is a fake or a delusion but just that it is too hard to
believe right now. For most people, a thing does not exist if
it cannot be grasped. It is easier to deny something than to
investigate it. But that is false reasoning, since the object of
research is to take the phenomenon first and then find the
best explanation for it.

Maharishi has said that science will not be able to explain
yogic flying until it takes consciousness into account. He has
taken many occasions to talk to physicists about this. As it

happens, the town of Seelisberg, where he was teaching the sidhis, is just a few hours' drive from CERN, the mammoth particle accelerator shared by several European nations. At one time or another, half of the leading quantum theorists in the world have talked to Maharishi, and at least one Nobel laureate is a meditator.

A physics model for yogic flying would start with Einstein, who had the intuition early in his career that natural laws should be the same for any observer in time and space. This insight led him to relativity and later to what he called "unified field theory," which means a single, unified explanation for all matter and energy in the universe. Einstein spent most of his later years working on the mathematical expression of a unified field but without success.

Since his death, considerable progress has been made by other physicists. What they have been moving toward is a level of nature's functioning where the apparent differences between matter and energy are abolished. So far, all the basic force and matter fields have in fact been unified, but gravity remains isolated. Until someone can theorize "supergravity," as it is called, it does not seem possible to make gravity behave like any other force in nature or to change it at all.

Maharishi feels that physics is getting advanced enough to explain yogic flying. He points out that the unified field, if it includes everything in the universe, can interact only with itself. Therefore, it has the property of consciousness. According to the Vedic texts, the whole of creation is nothing but consciousness interacting with itself. In a verse of the *Bhagavad-Gita* Krishna declares, "Curving back within myself, I create again and again." These words are literally describing how the unified field works, Maharishi says. A field of pure consciousness is curving back on itself to create everything in existence.

The British physicist Sir James Jeans had a flash of this when he wrote, "In the deeper reality beyond space and time, we may be all members of one body." So long as physics pays attention only to matter and energy, it will miss the deepest, most powerful agency of all, which is consciousness or intelligence. Only that will solve Einstein's dilemma, and only that will explain how man could move through the air using the force of thought.

Scientists, however, do not feel comfortable with this kind of reasoning. It is like telling someone who blasts granite with dynamite that you can do it just by thinking. So it may take a few more basic discoveries before physicists rally around yogic flying. T. H. Huxley, an eminent Victorian scientist, wrote an apt piece of advice in this regard: "Sit down before a fact, as a little child, be prepared to give up every preconceived notion, follow humbly wherever and to whatever abyss nature leads, or you shall learn nothing."

I didn't quote Huxley to the high school reporter. My answer to him was based on the logic of taking one step at a time. "Look, when you set out to drive from Boston to New York," I pointed out, "the signs at first don't say New York, do they? The first one says Providence, then the next one Hartford, and so on. If these are right, then you expect that the road will get to New York eventually. It's the same with flying. The signs are early, but they are all the right ones. I think we'll get there eventually." He said he could buy it.

The TM center in Cambridge sits in an imposing stucco house that was formerly used by Harvard as a center for foreign students. Three hours after the flying demonstration ended, a remote-location crew showed up from WBZ-TV, the NBC affiliate in Boston. The station had decided to run its "cover story" for the evening news on yogic flying. The report would last ten minutes, which amounted to sizable coverage. I was asked to appear for a live interview, which would be mixed in with taped material from the event itself.

I walked over the tangled cables onto the makeshift set that had been put together in the TM center's dining room. A pleasant young reporter named Jeanne Blake invited me to sit with her on a couch. We chatted for a second, then the lights went up and she turned to the camera.

I didn't know what angle she was going to take, but she indicated that the flying had looked very ambiguous to her. She seemed to imply that our six flyers might just have been bounding around using their muscles, although when she had tried to sit in lotus on the floor and hop, she hadn't moved an inch. Promptly at five-thirty the anchorman appeared on the monitor. With an amused expression he announced our story and turned to face Jeanne Blake's image projected in the studio.

"Looks like a real interesting story out there, Jeanne," he cued.

"It certainly is, Chris," she said. Now that we were on the air, she took a skeptical tack, not mentioning that she herself had tried to hop. The footage from our event looked impressive to me. The camera dwelt on the flyers trying to make the highest jump and failing — too bad. But that was offset by a number of good shots. During the taped segment, one of the flyers addressed the issue of fakery head-on: "The liftoff of the body is just a response to this mental technique. I'm sure you could get a professional gymnast to duplicate it, but then you wouldn't see the same pattern of brain wave coherence." As it happens, during the demonstration in Canada, a gymnast was invited to come on stage. He sat in full lotus and tried to hop. The TV coverage showed him sweating to move a few inches while the TM flyers blithely bounded around him 4 feet at a time without breathing hard.

As we came up for the live interview, Blake introduced Dr. William Polonsky, a clinical psychologist at Boston University's School of Medicine. In classic TV fashion, he was present to rebut our claims for the other side. His face, looking friendly and at ease, came up on the monitor. He seemed to be forty or so, about my age. I wondered to myself how he could possibly judge a ten-year program from watching ten minutes of tape in a studio.

"Dr. Polonsky, you saw what I saw. Is it flying or hopping?" Blake asked.

"It looks a lot like hopping to me," he replied. "I would not argue that meditation techniques, and specifically Transcendental Meditation, are effective in changing the physiology and promoting relaxation, perhaps even contributing to increased health. But that is separate from the question of whether it can help people to levitate. There is no evidence that I have seen to indicate that there has been any levitation."

"What would it take to make you a believer, Doctor?" the reporter asked.

"I'd have to see it," he replied. "I'd have to see people levitate."

"Dr. Polonsky," I interjected, "may I respond? You've been to magic shows, you've seen a lot of things. Do you believe all of them?"

"No, I don't," he said cautiously.

"Okay," I said, "so seeing is not believing, sir. It's the experience that gives one belief. You would have to have the experience yourself. You are a victim of your cultural indoctrination, that's all, like the rest of us."

As I was saying this, he tried to interrupt me, but I barreled along until Jeanne Blake cut me off and asked him to respond.

"I would disagree with you," he said. "I would say that seeing is the first stage of believing — and, again, we have not seen anything remotely resembling levitation or defying gravity. We have seen hopping. It's an interesting athletic skill, but —"

I had to jump in. "I feel it would be arrogant to say that we can defy gravity. Gravity holds all the planets together; it's one of the most powerful forces in nature. But we are saying that consciousness is an equally powerful force and that your perception is shaped by your experiences. Seeing is only one aspect of experience."

Blake wanted to wrap it up, but I leaned into the fray one more time. "And I think it's the height of arrogance to educate oneself with four or five years of medical school and three years of training, and then argue with a tradition that has existed unbroken for five thousand years."

At that point, we barely had time for the signoff. Dr. Polonsky's face, looking annoyed, disappeared from our monitor. And then we were off. The crew wrapped up their cables and broke down the set. Jeanne Blake bade me a friendly good-bye without asking anything else. I walked upstairs, where a small group of meditators had been watching the show. Most of the local flyers were at home doing their evening meditation. When I walked into the room, a few people standing around the TV applauded. One came over, beaming, to thump me on the chest. I could see that others were pensive. TM does not apply pressure to change people's opinions; for many years, the technique was not even commercially advertised. I had been a little more vociferous than anyone expected.

I congratulated everyone who organized the event, made a mental note to smooth the waters a little the next day, and got into my car to go home. On the way, I wondered how my patients would react. "My doctor is the one who thinks people can fly." Oh well.

I left the highway and caught one of the narrow roads overhung with oaks and maples leading to Lincoln, where I live. The way home is very pretty, really, once it gets into open countryside.

14

Soma

IF I WANTED to start farming, I could harvest the stars. I stopped one night on a desert road in India, the one that leads back from Maharishi Nagar to New Delhi. It was nearly three in the morning and I was alone. The same shadowy landscape lay in every direction around me, scrubby, flat, and dry. It seems peculiar, in a country as crowded as India, to think of there being empty places, but there are some, scoured clean by the angels and then forgotten. Getting out of my car, I listened for sounds in the night, for small, large-eyed animals or night-flying birds. There were none, or they were keeping still until I drove away. The darkness was so thick that I could not see the low red hills I knew were on the horizon.

The sights of this desert are all overhead. Leaning against the hood, I let my eyes sweep the rich fields of heaven. Summer stars, countless millions of them, twinkled in shimmers as the air rose up, radiating the heat of a scorching day. Squinting into the distance, I though I could still see the highest peak on the roof of the *kutiya,* or hut, where Maharishi lives. The building is larger than this humble word suggests.

Its lights stay in view for several miles as you make your way across the broad flatland. An hour before, I had been back there in the midst of roses and green arjuna trees. Several hundred of us had been sitting on the lawn, listening to one of Maharishi's nightly talks.

It was now 1986, about a year after Maharishi arrived back in India, nearly two since our first meeting in Washington. He had asked me to fly over this time to examine the progress being made on a new hospital he was planning to finish. His revival of Ayurveda, well under way in America, was returning to the land where Ayurveda was born. Three wings of the new hospital were projected; one of them already looked finished to the point where patients could start to come. I spent the day examining some advanced Western medical equipment — heart monitors, CAT scans, respirators, and X-rays. Disorders were to be treated according to Ayurveda, but these machines would serve as an adjunct, primarily so that Western doctors could verify the Ayurvedic methods by their own standards.

The first patients, many of them from the United States, came to India in serious condition, in some cases after everything at home had failed. I made rounds, visiting the rooms of several quite advanced cancer patients. It didn't seem completely fair to test Maharishi's Ayurveda on these terminal cases, but he is confident that results will be achieved once the vaidyas find the purest approach. That has always been Maharishi's main emphasis, that Ayurveda will be effective only after its purity is regained.

I was gratified to see that the patients looked better under the care they received here. The note of panic was gone from their voices, and the faces I looked into showed hope. The routine prescribed by the vaidyas already seemed helpful in easing chronic pain and restoring the body's strength after long illness had sapped it. The whole staff was pleased, including my father. He has now been meditating for several years and is very attached to Maharishi. He has agreed to come in from Delhi periodically to oversee the clinic here.

I filled my visit with medical work and meetings organized by Maharishi, but nothing I did in these areas accounts for the profound impression the place made on me. To call it a recuperative environment hardly does justice to Maharishi Nagar. Nowhere else has quite this purity. I overheard two English visitors talking about it at dinner. Like everyone, they felt that their experience here was special. After turning it over in their conversation, one ended by saying, "When I am here, something inside me melts." Yes.

Visiting Maharishi in his homeland is like returning to Bharata, the India of antiquity and light. Enlightenment came into existence in Bharata and fathered a culture. One sees its traces in the oldest images of art that have survived. So many of them depict the same unfading scene, of common people seated on the ground surrounding a great sage, a rishi. The sage appears to be delighting his rapt listeners with his words. He is talking about enlightenment, telling them that one day they will be perfect. He describes a path older than their memory and more permanent than the low, red hills they can see on the horizon. When he is through talking, they continue to sit with him, soaking up *soma*, the moonlight that Indian sages so love.

The wind has reclaimed its cities and is slowly wearing down its monuments, but we remember Bharata as the original India. Thanks to the survival of its wisdom, we also look upon it as the true India. Being around Maharishi now is like living in the ancestral images. I have seen a look from him that mirrors the merry, penetrating gaze of the old cave paintings. I have heard him break off in midsentence to murmur in pleasure at the moonlight as the evening breeze started up from the plain. It was just like the personal welcome we give a friend at the door. At that moment, wrapped in Maharishi's presence and the breathing of Nature, I remembered the beauty of living in innocence. No wonder that Maharishi has had to dig the wells deep. There have been thousands of visitors already who took time to come and learn.

People are still eager to hear about enlightenment. All day, hour after hour, and well into the night after I was asleep, the doctors, academics, vaidyas, and pundits came to talk. Besides the Indians, a great many Americans regularly make the journey here — sixteen hours by jet, not counting the unpredictable bus ride from Delhi. But you can also hear Latin Americans talking in small groups at meals and see African faces pass by.

These people come from poorer societies, where it is likely that Western medical technology will never be affordable. In certain ways, they are fortunate in this regard. I once heard a government minister in India boast about flying to Houston for his heart bypass graft, as though that was a status symbol. If it were left up to him, or to most Westernized Indians, the hardware of modern medicine would have the top priority in the national health budget and Ayurveda the bottom — which is actually almost the case now. They are shocked when doctors like me return home to declare that Ayurveda can make India a leader in the medicine of the future, particularly for the developing nations.

Maharishi holds out to these nationalities an alluring prospect: Transcendental Meditation and Ayurvedic medicine can become the core of health care anywhere and are affordable even in the poorest countries. As Maharishi presents it, Ayurveda complements the existing traditional medicine in every locale around the world. It can re-enliven these traditions, which are nearly extinct in all but a few societies, by restoring the techniques and preparations that have been lost, making each system whole once more.

That essentially means making all of them Ayurveda once more. I am reminded that Ayurveda is not "Indian medicine" — it is a universal medicine that fortunately has survived in India. Who knows how far the vaidyas will reach out? Dr. Triguna has toured many countries, including China and Brazil, two areas where strong aspects of Ayurveda still remain. There he offers Ayurveda, not as a substitute, but as a senior partner. Maharishi has also asked me to present Ayurveda abroad, including talks to the leading medical association of Egypt and the World Health Organization in Switzerland. We are in serious pursuit of a medicine for mankind.

I could tell on my visits to Maharishi Nagar that remarkable people from India have also been attracted to hear Maharishi. The wholeness of Vedic knowledge is no longer present throughout India, but lively fragments still exist and are embodied in a few figures. Maharishi shows an intense interest in them. He says that they are really the last to survive — after this generation, much of the pure knowledge will be lost. To avert such a calamity, he is scouring the country for all these living treasures.

On this particular visit in 1986, we heard from Trigunaji, who is one of them, and also from a new discovery. One evening in the garden we were introduced to Dr. Balraj Maharshi, an authority on Ayurvedic herbs. He was a monk, dressed in the traditional white dhoti, a modest man who rarely contributed to discussions. Even so, one easily sensed his spiritual depth. He devoted the earlier part of his life to studies with a Himalayan master and was secluded with him for twenty years. Now he knows the curative properties of several thousand plants. Hundreds of them are said to be known by no one else in the whole of Ayurveda, or at most by a handful of recluses. More than that, Dr. Balraj Maharshi has the ability described in the classical Ayurvedic texts of knowing an herb's medicinal qualities simply from looking at it. Maharishi is obviously delighted with him and hopes that he can start herb gardens for Ayurveda around the world, using every country's local plants. Balraj says confidently that this is possible.

I witnessed a remarkable demonstration of Balraj's abilities at home. At our Ayurvedic center in Massachusetts we were presented with the case of Paulina, an eight-year-old girl who is mentally retarded. She was evaluated according to Ayurvedic procedure; Balraj then prescribed a special leaf that was to be boiled in a cup of milk. He explained to us that this particular herb was a cousin of the soma plant.

To anyone who has looked into the Vedas, this is a startling claim. "Soma" is the name of both the moon and its light, but also much more than that. In a subtler form, it is considered to be the primordial substance out of which the created world began. It therefore instills the qualities common to creation — wholeness, intelligence, well-being, and bliss. Soma is revered, and entire books of the Veda are devoted to glorifying it. One mark of an enlightened man is that his own body produces soma, but there is also a plant from which it can be extracted.

No agreement exists about the identity of the soma plant. Balraj himself says that it is extremely rare but not legendary. He has seen it three times in his life. Its entire life cycle, fittingly enough, is tied to the moon. On the day of the new moon it has no leaves. One leaf sprouts each day after this, until by the arrival of the full moon there are fifteen leaves. And then the cycle reverses. The soma plant sheds its leaves, one by one, until by the next new moon it is once again entirely bare. Balraj says that the powers of its leaves are so great that simply to look upon the soma plant creates bliss in the beholder.

Naturally, we were extremely fascinated to hear this story, and plans were drawn up in India to send a field expedition to the Himalayas to attempt to find such a plant. For the time being, Balraj offered us this related herb, which has only a Sanskrit name. It looks like a leaf from the arrowroot family, however, pointed and curled up into a cylinder in its dried state. One of the vaidyas informed me that the leaf is discouraged in its dried form, because it has so far failed to help a human being. However, he said, it will be very happy to give its essence up when it is put into hot milk. Indeed, when we steeped the leaf, it took only a few minutes for the dried cylinder to unroll, swell up, and turn bright green again, almost like a freshly picked leaf. As Balraj recommended, we gave a little of the milk to our patient, little Paulina, every day for a week. At the end, after she went home with a supply of the leaf, her parents called with remarkable news. Their daughter was showing progress in very unexpected ways. I took notes one morning when her mother spoke to me that week:

"In the past, Paulina has never been able to express herself very well or to understand others. Now I can't believe how well she is understanding us. I am very excited. So is her pediatrician; he tells us he wants to do formal tests. I have not mentioned this to anyone, because I don't want to give lengthy explanations, but I have a background in clinical psychology myself, and I know what I am seeing. But even more so, I see the difference because I am her mother.

"Paulina has never been able to draw a person before, only scribbles, but now she draws people, and the drawings look beautiful, even though they are rudimentary. Her verbal expression has also improved, along with her short-term memory. I see a clinical improvement, moving from primitive development to integrative. A babysitter who had not seen her for three months came over the other day and said that the changes in Paulina are amazing.

"I do not get myself too hopeful. I feel that I am hopeful without expectations. More than anything else, I am just grateful for the healing that is taking place in my own heart."

The center where we saw Paulina is in Lancaster, Massachusetts, near Boston, on a grand estate. The mansion itself was long uninhabited as a house and was large enough to convert into a fair-size clinic. The surrounding two hundred and ten acres give us seclusion. Beneath a tangle of woodbine and Virginia creeper, you can discern the outlines of clogged marble fountains. No one knows exactly how many there are — we have found half a dozen already.

Our medical facility here is comparable to what Maharishi is constructing in India, but on a smaller scale. Almost all the people who presently come for Ayurvedic treatment are meditators. They undertake Ayurveda as part of a seasonal routine for maintaining health and also to promote the best possible inner experiences. Ayurveda can actually provide deepened awareness because it makes no firm distinction between the body and the psyche: balancing the physical system affects both. Another proportion of our patients, few of them meditators, come to us with developed diseases. Sometimes they have been diagnosed as fatal; otherwise, they are advanced degenerative disorders that conventional medicine has not relieved.

In this second group was Mr. Diaz, seventy years old and a senior member of a powerful Latin American family, which means that he was wealthy enough to fly to the United States for care. When I first saw him, the day he arrived in this country, it was obvious that he was a very sick man. He was carrying 170 pounds on a 5'4" frame that should have carried closer to 135 pounds. Because of extremely high blood pressure, his heart was beginning to back up fluid into his lungs — a condition called congestive heart failure — and even sitting up caused him to wheeze.

Because his heart condition was serious, Mr. Diaz had been put on maximum medication to bring down his blood pressure, but it was not helping. I could see that he might have heart failure soon. It was not surprising to find that quite a few other things had gone wrong in his body. His digestion was bad because of ballooning pockets in his colon, or diverticulosis. These pockets collected toxins from his digestive tract as food passed through and became painfully inflamed. His prostate had also swollen, making it painful for him to pass urine.

Mr. Diaz was sent to our Lancaster clinic for this variety of disorders that he could not cope with, but there was really only one thing that could help him — his body's inner intelligence, which Ayurveda defines as the organizing power that flows from its deep source in the self and coordinates every aspect of the physical system. Although he was very sick, Mr. Diaz had not lost this intelligence. He had certainly not been in touch with it for a long time, or he would not have been in the shape that he was in.

Mr. Diaz was living in a body of his own making. He had created this body and its unbalanced condition; he then took medication to offset the mistakes being made inside. He further complicated matters by drugging himself to compensate for the side effects of the medicines he took, side effects that included fatigue, impaired thinking, and sexual impotence. Some of his medications, in fact, had been prescribed for no other reason than to offset the undesirable effects of previous medications.

I put him immediately on the most intensive Ayurvedic plan, including learning to meditate. Mr. Diaz spoke English well enough so that I could give him a pep talk. It came straight from Ayurveda, but with no special jargon.

I said, "While you are here, our goal should not be to fight disease but to restore you to happiness. You are not happy now because you have lost self-control. Your body is your choice. You have created this diseased body that you now have. You can create a healthy body using the same ability. Given the right guidance, your body can reset itself, even if it has almost gone over the brink already. It's finally up to you. No one else can create a new body for you but yourself."

This approach began to pay off in a remarkably short time. His body's inner intelligence just had not had a chance to help him. He had been too busy creating so many problems for himself. We didn't even have to do all that much. The philosophy of Ayurveda is to do the minimum — simply remove the inner obstacles and let Nature do the rest.

By putting him on the correct Ayurvedic diet, reducing his salt and fat intake to nearly zero, and getting him to meditate, we made Mr. Diaz feel much better right away. All sorts of things began to happen for him: he lost 10 pounds, his congestive heart failure was dramatically alleviated, his blood pressure dropped to 110 over 70 — lower than any reading he had ever seen since he was an adolescent. Instead of wheezing when he sat up, he began to enjoy a brisk half-hour walk in the morning. He told us how much he loved the New England foliage as it was turning its brilliant fall colors. Because he felt energetic and much more alive, he began to lengthen his walks to an hour. The exercise and fresh air brought a glow to his skin, and for the first time his body looked vital.

Clinically, we found it possible to taper off the medications for the high blood pressure; by the end of his two-week stay, they were far below maximum levels, and we hoped that soon he would be off all of them. His digestion had normalized, so the diverticulosis was no longer such a problem. His swollen prostate improved by at least 50 percent, down from 30 percent obstruction to 15 percent. This came as an enormous relief to Mr. Diaz, since his doctors at home had told him that he must have immediate prostate surgery.

After his stay, Mr. Diaz was tremendously enthusiastic. He had arrived knowing nothing about Ayurveda or the principles behind it, but some simple interventions directed to diet and daily routine turned his health around. If he continued on his program, there was every chance that he would improve even more. His body was once again the result of his own choice.

Whenever patients come who are not meditators, we encourage them to bring friends along who have some experience with TM and the other unique things, like *panchakarma*, that our center offers. One young couple named Annie and Michael Wyler came in that capacity very soon after the facility opened, escorting a retired couple from the Midwest.

Now that they were in their sixties, a number of illnesses were setting in that made the older couple interested in Ayurveda. Both husband and wife had been diagnosed by Dr. Triguna on one of his trips to America, but neither knew much about TM or Maharishi's revival of Ayurveda. As long-term meditators, the Wylers could act as a buffer to so many new experiences, and at the same time they could take a week of Ayurveda for themselves.

Everything went extremely well, but the older couple was still timid about being in such an unaccustomed environment. One night I decided to sleep over, just so that they would feel a little more reassured. The mansion originally had some forty-five bedrooms; I took one in the wing nearest theirs. Ayurveda prescribes warm milk with a teaspoon of melted butter in it before bedtime. We had ours together, and then everyone went to bed. It was about ten o'clock.

Some time later I heard banging at my door. Barely awake, I went to open it and saw Michael Wyler. He looked very pale and distraught. I could see that he was shaking.

"I think Annie is dead," he whispered. We rushed to their room down the hallway. Another resident doctor was already on hand, bending over Annie's body. She was lying in bed, showing no movement and apparently no breath. Her skin had begun to turn blue, a sign that oxygen was not being taken into her system. Everything seemed at a standstill. I wondered why emergency procedures had not been started already. The other doctor looked over and told me that she was beginning to show signs of coming out of her coma. He could just then detect very faint and irregular breathing. We had a few minutes to spare, so I asked her husband to describe as carefully as he could what had happened.

He told us that he had been reading in bed when he noticed Annie's hand beginning to tremble. She was asleep at the time, but the trembling grew more agitated and moved up her arm. In a minute or two her whole body was thrashing. He tried to hold her down. She did not wake up, but in a short while the movements stopped abruptly, her eyes rolled upward, and she fell into a coma. Thinking that she could be dead, Michael had called for help and rushed to fetch me.

The other doctor and I agreed that he had described what is known as a Jacksonian seizure. Usually it is idiopathic, which means that doctors can find no direct cause for it. We were discussing what to do next when Annie began to breathe more regularly and then to open her eyes.

As is usually the case in such seizures, she did not know that anything unusual had happened and had no memory of the episode. Seeing us standing around her bed in a state of alarm obviously bewildered her. She started to question us. Fortunately, an Ayurvedic vaidya appeared on the scene as a distraction, offering herbal tea. That, and our repeated reassurances, somewhat calmed her fears. Michael was still extremely distressed, but after a while we all were able to return to our rooms.

The next morning I explained the medical situation to both of them. I advised Annie to go to a Boston hospital for cranial X-rays. The chances of anything abnormal appearing were minor, I assured them. The Wylers were willing to do as I advised, but Michael took me aside before they left.

"You think it's a brain tumor, don't you?" he said. He was almost as distraught as he had been the night before. I told him that I didn't think that at all; in fact, the chances of a tumor appearing without any prior symptoms in a young, healthy woman were quite small. He still looked very upset as he left for the city.

The next day I received a call from the radiology department of the best hospital in Boston. They were sorry to inform me, but Mrs. Wyler's X-rays disclosed a shadow that was consistent with a diagnosis of brain tumor. A cancer specialist had examined the pictures. He could not be expected to commit himself at such an early stage, but he strongly suspected that the tumor was malignant. Its present size and character also led him to think that it had spread from another part of the body. The patient was advised to undergo immediate surgery to remove the tumor and to determine definitely whether it was cancerous or not.

I rushed to the hospital and confronted the Wylers, almost as much in shock as they were. If the tumor had spread from another part of the body, there was very little hope. Michael had been shattered by the news. Annie, though naturally upset, did not accept the worst.

"There must be something on the X-rays," she conceded, "but I don't have a brain tumor." I told her that every doctor involved — and all of them were extremely experienced — had interpreted her X-rays the same way. She listened quietly, but she still repeated her conviction — she didn't have a tumor. I left the Wylers feeling more than discouraged. The shadow of a doubt had fallen over me, and though we didn't speak openly about it, I'm sure they felt the same. They were young, happy, and healthy. They meditated, practiced the TM-Sidhis, and devoted a great deal of time and money to Maharishi's teachings. I had heard him in India repeatedly emphasizing that in the field of consciousness, there is infinite choice. To be well was a choice, and so was becoming sick.

So how could this disastrous choice happen to Annie? Didn't the precepts we knew about consciousness amount to something certain, a sort of guarantee that the right choices had been made? We all knew that thinking this way was too simple in the face of our inner complexity, but most people who knew the Wylers, probably even their families, would be following the same line of reasoning. Annie's situation seemed like a betrayal.

I went back to my practice. The next two days were filled with work, and when I was handed a message that I should call Maharishi Nagar in India, I put it off. The Wylers stayed in communication up to the point where Annie went into surgery. I left instructions to be called as soon as the pathologist had determined whether the tumor was malignant or benign. At five in the afternoon the news came.

It wasn't the surgeon but Michael on the line, and he sounded extremely excited. Annie did not have cancer. In fact, she did not have a tumor. The shadow on her X-rays had been caused by an AV malformation. Michael didn't quite know what that meant, but it had been removed and his wife was out of danger. Now I was much more excited than he. An AV (arterial-venous) malformation is extremely rare. It is a tangle of small blood vessels that forms in the brain when the arteries and veins in one area do not become connected by capillaries as they normally do. An AV malformation is much more fragile than the correct formation of vessels, and therein lies its great danger. At some point in the patient's lifetime, generally without warning, the malformed vessels rupture. The result, as with any cerebral hemorrhage, is serious — usually severe brain damage or even death.

I had been on an elevator once with a friend, a fellow medical student in India, who complained of having a sudden headache. The next moment, he dropped to the floor. He had died instantly, and when the autopsy came out, it showed the cause of death to be an AV malformation. Like Annie, he had no idea beforehand that it existed. In her case, the vessels had ruptured and caused her seizure, but then they had spontaneously stopped bleeding. She was incredibly fortunate. Now that the malformation had been removed, she was out of danger. She could lead a completely normal life with no threat of further incidents.

I found the Wylers in Annie's hospital room. Michael was overjoyed. Annie lay back on her pillow, exhausted from the surgery. Her head was bandaged and part of her hair had been shaved off for the operation, but she looked radiant. Her mind was just beginning to take in what had happened.

"It can't all be a coincidence," she insisted. "If Triguna hadn't seen our friends, and we hadn't come with them to Lancaster, what would have happened to me? I might have had a seizure driving the car, and then I would probably be dead. But I was at the clinic at the right time, the hemorrhaging stopped by itself, and the whole chain of events led me here, just to this moment. These things don't just happen."

She was saying what the rishis say in a phrase: "Reality is only consciousness." The inner intelligence knows how to shape events, and at critical moments, their significance comes through. I thought of how intimate one's evolution is, and with what power it can suddenly advance. In place of so many small steps, there is suddenly one breathtaking stride.

Annie looked like someone set free. She and Michael were both transformed by their happiness. The expression on their faces said, "Look! We've come through." The atmosphere around them was brighter, and for the remaining week of their stay it remained like that. Annie's sense of triumph swept us all up. I had never felt happier for a patient.

I got home very late and went to bed, much more exhausted than I had realized. Rita would be very happy in the morning when I told her about Annie. After midnight the phone rang. It was India on the line, and across the usual garbled connection I gathered that I was talking to another doctor. Then I recognized his voice — it was Dr. Mahapatra, a cancer specialist who spends time at Maharishi's clinic, helping to follow patients.

"We've been trying to get you for two days," he said. "Didn't you get our messages?" I decided it would be easier all around just to say no.

"The Wylers contacted us," he went on. "They wanted to come to the hospital here. We're not really clear about what they expected, but Maharishi doesn't want them to be upset. That's why I'm calling. They don't need to come to India."

"No?" I said.

"Maharishi asked me yesterday to tell them that everything will be all right. He says that Annie doesn't have a tumor. Can you pass that on to her?"

I held on to the receiver in silence. A reproachful thought crossed my mind: if I had called India sooner, I might have alleviated two days of tension and misery for all of us.

"Hello?" the voice on the other end asked. "Still there?"

"Yes, thanks. Listen, we're all right now, and very happy. It's turned out well." I sketched in the day's events, then added my thanks once more and said good-bye. Going back to bed, I noticed how cool the night air was. I stood at a window, feeling the faint current of breeze move across me, like a breath.

So Maharishi knew, the same as Annie. But what about her physician? Shouldn't I be standing on the same ground with them, sharing the same awareness? Of course I should. I wasn't enough of a rishi to be able to do that, but I wanted to.

I looked out the window at the crescent moon. It was like a sickle in the sky, harvesting stars in the rich fields of heaven. Everything around me shared its beauty. I stood and marveled, wrapped in the presence of soma — a silent moon sailing homeward to India, but at home over America tonight.

Postscript

I WAS ALONE when I learned that Jawaharlal Nehru was dead. My father had gone on a posting to Kashmir, and since I was still in high school, I stayed behind to live in Delhi with my uncle. He was not at home that afternoon as I stood in shock next to the radio, my lunch forgotten on the kitchen table.

It would be impossible to describe the desolation I felt or the wave of grief that passed through the collective soul of India. Nehru had been our father. People would pick up a rose he had tossed from his car during a procession and cherish it for life. At school that year, 1964, I read Shakespeare, Dickens, and Nehru's book *The Discovery of India*. When my uncle came home, we immediately joined the cortege that was following the body as it proceeded to the burning ghats on the banks of the Ganges. Literally millions of Indians made that walk, but each person in it walked alone.

At the Ganges we saw the flames leap up from an enormous funeral pyre. The limp flags borne by the color guard wavered in the unbearable heat of a summer day in Delhi. I remember the troops mounted on camels, sitting bolt upright at attention, and the women weeping behind veils. Uncle and I sat down and wept with them.

By the next morning, Nehru's ashes had been gathered and placed in state on the veranda of his house, Teen Murti. Once again I went with my uncle to file past, but the scene had already shifted. Police lines had been drawn, guarded by policemen carrying billy clubs. People in the crowd jostled each other impatiently. I felt that I was close to being crushed several times, but after two hours we finally drew up to the veranda.

The ashes had been put into a small, very plain earthen jar. Neither my uncle nor I was crying. In a bitter voice, my uncle muttered, "He was everything yesterday, but what is Nehru now?"

Our lives seem arranged to remind us of change and its sorrows. You do not have to follow the body of a great man to feel this — walking down the corridor of a suburban hospital is good enough. Sickness, war, old age, and death remind us of it repeatedly. In order not to feel that everything I cherish stands on sand, I turned to medicine for solutions. But the perplexities of life are too disturbing. They are not solved simply by dissecting a ten-rupee brain or by learning all the other bits and pieces of modern medicine, either.

Because the scene shifts every second of every day, life does stand on sand. But we have the choice to plant our feet in the universe. That is Ayurveda's revelation. Consciousness is primary to our existence, and in meditation one discovers it to be the one unchanging part of life. It turned into the first impulse of intelligence contained in the first cell that became you and me, no more than a flicker of life at the moment of conception and yet containing the total information of the universe.

Ayurveda says this: "Pay attention to that unchanging part of yourself. It is perfect. At the source of life, and only there, one finds peace, harmony, and the undisturbed contentment of bliss." This message has thrilled all who have heard it in the past, and it will continue to thrill men so long as the Ayurvedic knowledge endures.

I have not gone into the multifold details of Ayurvedic procedures because I wanted to throw the sharpest possible focus on the personal lessons I have learned. Our current beliefs about reality would exclude many of the things touched on in this book. But disbelief can loosen its hold, and then reality leaps into a vastly larger scale. On this vastly larger scale, beneath the diversity evident to our senses, lies one wholeness. We cannot comprehend this deeper reality with bits of our perception. It can only be touched through the mechanism of transcendence. Separation, fragmentation, fear, insecurity, hostility, result because we have lost touch with this continuum of life that is the source of all creation. When we are there, we realize that the Self, the rishi, is no other than this unity, and this unity is no other than the Self. With this realization comes compassion. With compassion comes love, and with love comes peace.

This must happen if we are to solve the problems that we have created. It took our diseased thoughts to create our imperfect world. Now, as the cure, we must learn to see other people in the light of love. When love rises in us, it will rise in the world as a whole. A new reality will be apparent that is laid on a foundation of health, happiness, and personal freedom. Ayurveda offers these as gifts, if only we are not so blind as to reject them.

I see glimpses of this future every day, treating patients at Lancaster. Even the most seriously ill look at me with the light that only deep silence and purity can bring. I hope every doctor has the privilege of taking up the responsibility that Ayurveda places in the hands of the physician. To make people well, according to Ayurveda, means to make them perfect. This is not a distant goal. With the proper guidance, anyone can be set on the path to perfection simply by knowing the self. When the eternal knower, the rishi, wakes up in anyone, it proclaims, "I must survive, I must create, I must be." That marks the moment when human life truly begins.

That is the challenge of this book.

About the Author

Deepak Chopra, M.D., has practiced endocrinology since 1971 and is former chief of staff of New England Memorial Hospital, Stoneham, Massachusetts.

In 1985 he became the founding president of the American Association of Ayurvedic Medicine and is now medical director of the Maharishi Ayurveda Health Center for Stress Management and Behavioral Medicine, in Lancaster, Massachusetts.

Dr. Chopra lectures widely on Ayurveda and health in the United States and abroad. He has addressed audiences from U.S. medical schools to the World Health Organization in Geneva, and the United Nations in New York. His first book, *Creating Health: Beyond Prevention, Toward Perfection* (Houghton Mifflin), was honored by the National Press Club as a book of international significance.

He lives in Lincoln, Massachusetts, with his wife, Rita, and two children, Mallika and Gautama.